PAUL McCARTNEY
AND WINGS

Tony Jasper

CHARTWELL
BOOKS INC.

CONTENTS

First published in the USA 1977 by Chartwell Books, Inc.,
a division of Book Sales, Inc.
110 Enterprise Avenue, Secaucus, New Jersey 07094
© 1977 Octopus Books Limited

ISBN 0-7064-0663-X

Printed in Great Britain by
Severn Valley Press, Caerphilly, Glamorgan

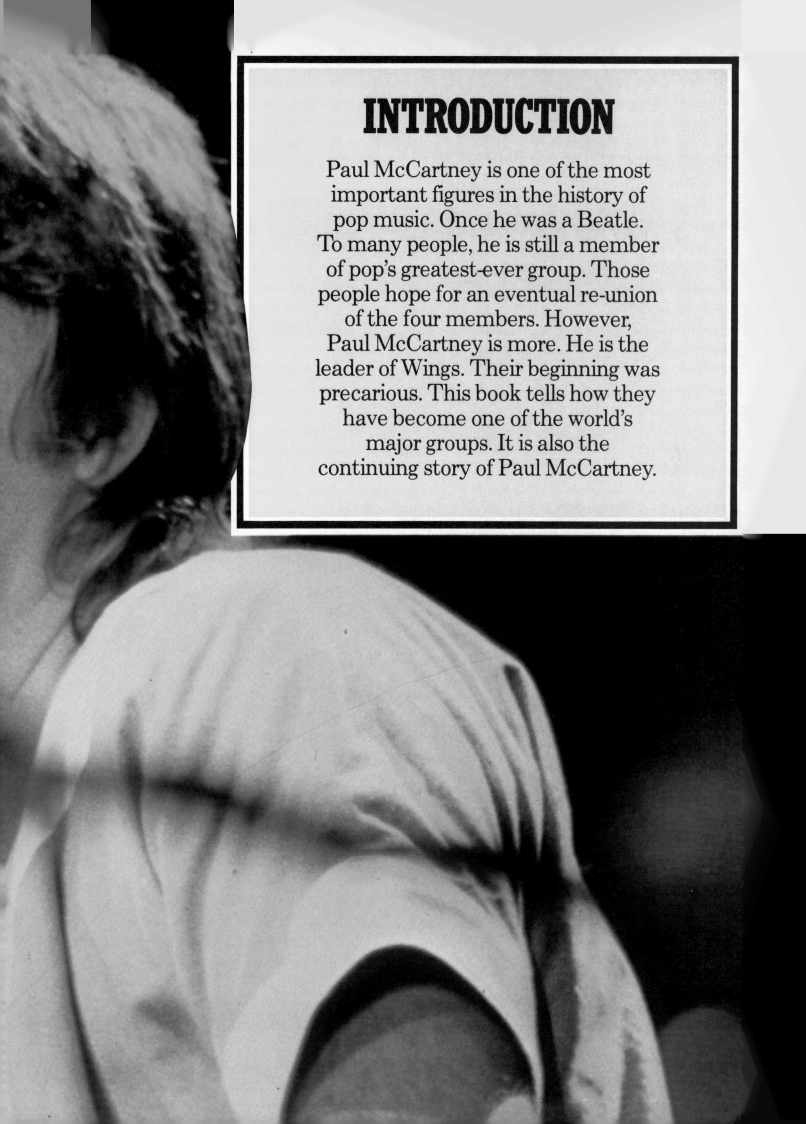

INTRODUCTION

Paul McCartney is one of the most important figures in the history of pop music. Once he was a Beatle. To many people, he is still a member of pop's greatest-ever group. Those people hope for an eventual re-union of the four members. However, Paul McCartney is more. He is the leader of Wings. Their beginning was precarious. This book tells how they have become one of the world's major groups. It is also the continuing story of Paul McCartney.

"Really, I try to lead a pretty normal life. The only abnormality is being Paul McCartney." Quoted in *Melody Maker* January 15, 1977.

"A swarm of near-hysterical fans in a shrieking stamping, jumping crowd around the stage at the end of the concert revived memories of the Beatles in their heyday"—report from the Wings World Tour, Zoltan Kovacs, *The West Australian* November 3, 1975

"Wings are not famed for their sheer musical adventurousness, more for getting everything in place and doing it right, and this is the effect that comes across here." Comment on Wings and **Wings Over America** in *Album Tracking*, January, 1977.

"Paul's a great artist, incredibly creative, incredibly clever"—Ringo Starr to *Melody Maker*, July 31, 1971.

"I don't think we can expect anything deep or significant from him because he's just not that kind of artist. But good pop, yes, I'm sure we can expect that." Stephen Barnard, *Let It Rock*. March, 1974.

"If a typical pop group exists it must be very dull. Wings certainly isn't typical; how could it be, with the legendary figure of Paul McCartney at the helm?"—Dave Gelly, *Introduction to The Facts About A Pop Group*—featuring Wings.

"Our love life has nothing to do with it, because when you're in love, and this goes for Paul and Linda too, when you're in love nothing else is really important."—John Lennon on The Beatle split and relations with Paul in *Rolling Stone*. May 10, 1973.

"Since then the music and life-styles of the four ex-Beatles have grown more and more widely divergent . . . Paul McCartney is doing it with Wings . . ." Charles Shaar Murray, *New Musical Express*, May 5, 1973.

"The days of ex-Beatledom and ex-Moody (Denny Laine) are numbered while the advent of Wings is only just beginning to show. That's what Paul says any-way."—Peter Harvey in *Record Mirror*, July 21, 1973.

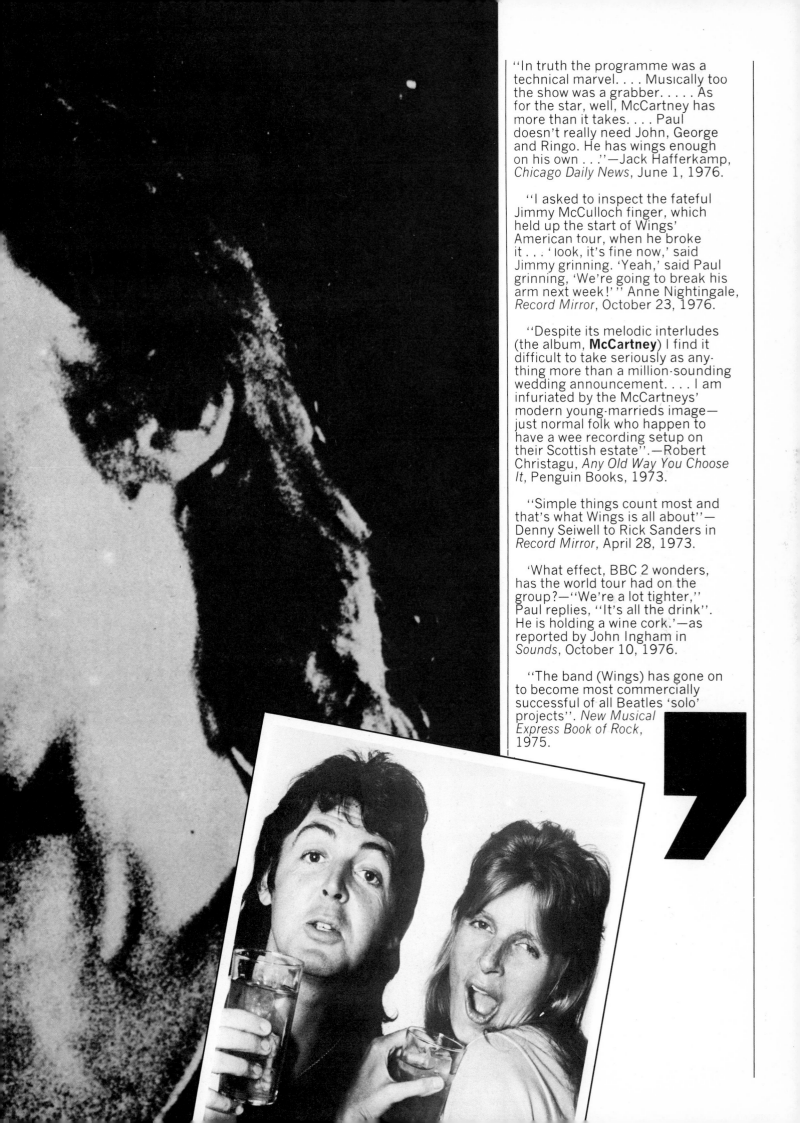

"In truth the programme was a technical marvel. . . . Musically too the show was a grabber. . . . . As for the star, well, McCartney has more than it takes. . . . Paul doesn't really need John, George and Ringo. He has wings enough on his own . . ."—Jack Hafferkamp, *Chicago Daily News*, June 1, 1976.

"I asked to inspect the fateful Jimmy McCulloch finger, which held up the start of Wings' American tour, when he broke it . . . 'look, it's fine now,' said Jimmy grinning. 'Yeah,' said Paul grinning, 'We're going to break his arm next week!'" Anne Nightingale, *Record Mirror*, October 23, 1976.

"Despite its melodic interludes (the album, **McCartney**) I find it difficult to take seriously as any-thing more than a million-sounding wedding announcement. . . . I am infuriated by the McCartneys' modern young-marrieds image— just normal folk who happen to have a wee recording setup on their Scottish estate".—Robert Christagu, *Any Old Way You Choose It*, Penguin Books, 1973.

"Simple things count most and that's what Wings is all about"— Denny Seiwell to Rick Sanders in *Record Mirror*, April 28, 1973.

'What effect, BBC 2 wonders, has the world tour had on the group?—"We're a lot tighter," Paul replies, "It's all the drink". He is holding a wine cork.'—as reported by John Ingham in *Sounds*, October 10, 1976.

"The band (Wings) has gone on to become most commercially successful of all Beatles 'solo' projects". *New Musical Express Book of Rock*, 1975.

1
THE FORMATION OF WINGS

On April 10, 1970, Paul McCartney announced his declaration of independence from the Beatles and the world press decided this was the end for the group. Six months later Paul sued the other three group members. For fans of the fabulous four this action only confirmed suspicions that J.P. McCartney was indeed the naughty boy. They thought that he alone had destroyed the greatest outfit ever seen or heard on disc and it took some people years to see that McCartney's move had been necessary. Someone had to admit that the Beatles as a group had fallen apart and do something about it.

The split in the Beatles camp did not occur on April 10 nor December 30 nor during the lengthy court wrangles. Tensions within the group can be traced as far back as **Let It Be**, some would go further. Certainly, the album **Abbey Road** saw the four working happily together in a recording studio. But those who would cast Paul McCartney as the villain conveniently forgot

Lennon's own unconventional life-style developing with Yoko Ono, the subsequent wedding, the much-publicized honeymoon and the wedding album. It was Lennon who formed the Plastic Ono Band while the Beatles were still officially in existence, and even if the disc **Live Peace In Toronto** was a good one it hardly helped keep the Beatles together.

Paul McCartney's role in the break-up of the Beatles was exaggerated in an extraordinary interview John Lennon gave in the American rock music journal, *Rolling Stone*. Tony Tyler, once Editor of the British musical paper, *The New Musical Express*, described Lennon with the adjective 'wretched'. In his view Lennon had taken every opportunity to blame McCartney, suggesting that the Beatle break in some part was caused by a Paul who was purely concerned with Linda and rearing chickens and sheep on his Scottish farm. In an interview with another British musical paper, *Melody Maker*, Lennon even took the group's dissention back into the era of manager Brian Epstein. He said that when it came to the question of dress, it was Brian and Paul who had insisted on neat suits and shirts. Lennon on this occasion said, 'My little rebellion was to have my tie loose, with the top button of my shirt undone, but Paul would always come up to me and put it straight.'

Doubtless many hasty words were spoken and were later regretted. The four Beatles were all pursuing their separate interests and none more than John Lennon. He went to live in New York and it was he who attracted the newspaper headlines and who became for a time the rock world's leading political propagandist. An inkling of the ideas in which Lennon found himself more and more engrossed can be gleaned from these words he spoke to *Rolling Stone*, April 16, 1970, 'Someone said, "Do We need a Festival?" Yoko and I still think we need it (he is referring to the then proposed Toronto Peace Festival), not just to show that we can gather peacefully and groove to rock bands, but to change the balance of energy power on earth and, therefore, in the universe.'

While John forged ahead with his peace campaign, Paul McCartney only became unemployed. He wasn't short of money, but, as he remarked later, he felt himself to be unemployed in the psychological sense, with his main occupation gone and no clear view of

Together for the last time. The Beatles played on the roof of London's Apple building but, although the song was **Get Back,** they were all going their separate ways. John Lennon and Yoko Ono travelled to North America to publicize their message of peace with stunts like the 'bag in' and the 'bed in'. Their Plastic Ono Band was the first breakaway group and put Lennon potentially in the category of ex-Beatle.

his future. Still Paul had Linda; the two had married on March 12, 1969. But even that obviously happy event for Paul failed to please many Beatle fans, even some of those whose favourite Paul was.

Paul decided that his future lay in solo work. So he began working on his own album. It was issued under the title **McCartney** on April 17, 1970, seven days after Paul's momentous declaration of independence.

Paul McCartney's brother-in-law, New York attorney John Eastman, who had taken charge of Paul's business affairs since Paul opposed the introduction by the others of Allen Klein to clear up the financial mess of the Apple empire, issued the press with a prepared statement. It said that Paul had formed his own production company and he would be pursuing ventures independent of the other three Beatles. Paul would not be recording any further Beatle material and he was not represented by Klein. There were several impolite remarks made of John and Ringo and of prime importance the statement of his break with the Beatles.

However, the break with the rest of the group was not a simple matter for, although Allen Klein did not represent Paul, there was still the point that all the Beatles had a contract with Apple Corporation. The ramifications of this were worked out in the ensuing court and out-of-court wrangles. Paul's solo album appeared on the Apple label but when American review copies were mailed out from John Eastman's office, the address of Apple's New York City office, also that of Allen Klein, was covered over by a strip of black tape. John Lennon accused Paul of causing chaos because he couldn't have his own way. He talked of Beatle-sulking Paul. Paul's resignation was not popular.

There was more controversy to come. Three weeks after **McCartney** was issued, the controversial **Let It Be** L.P. was issued by Apple. Some people saw it as an attempt at squashing Paul's first solo offering while others merely saw it as an unfortunate or even unwise release date. Paul at first thought that the others were deliberately trying to wreck his album but later he saw things differently. Nevertheless there was a story which said Ringo was sent by the other two around to Paul's London home with the purpose of smoothing things over, and was thrown out of the house.

The album **Let It Be** contained material which Paul found somewhat

March 12, 1969. Paul married Linda Eastman at Marylebone Register Office. He had hurriedly bought the ring the day before for £12, knocking up the jeweller, who had closed for the night. Best man was Paul's brother Mike. Linda's daughter by her previous marriage, Heather, was present at the ceremony. Asked whether she was a member of the wealthy Eastman photographic family, Linda replied no. 'What?' said Paul. 'I've been done! Where's the money?'

irritating. **Let It Be** had three producers. In the first place there was George Martin and he was assisted by Glyn Johns. Their work was apparently not well received and the recording tapes, some thirty hours in all, were stored away, though one story says Johns was asked to do some further remixing. Eventually they were released from hibernation and American producer Phil Spector was given the task of re-editing, re-mixing and eventually coming up with a finished set of album tracks. Spector is renowned for his favourite pastime of embellishing material with lavish orchestral elaborations. One song he chose for such treatment was Paul's The **Long And Winding Road**. Spector said he had the agreement of all the Beatles on the finished work but Paul has always denied that he was consulted on this particular song. It seemed, he did not appreciate what is on **Let It Be**; indeed a very different-sounding version of **The Long And Winding Road** can be heard on certain 'bootleg' discs.

Paul's **McCartney** was very much a one-man effort. Paul played all the instruments and his only outside help was by Linda who contributed toward the harmonies. He said his taste in music hadn't changed because he was no longer a Beatle; in fact he was still pursuing the same kind of musical path. Music reviews of **McCartney** were hardly flattering and to many people only one high-class song came from the L.P. – **Maybe I'm Amazed**.

Paul had one more solo album released before he finally formed a band. The disc was **Ram** with its date of issue, May 21, 1971. Three months later came Wings. **Ram** did little to enhance Paul's reputation. It seemed light-weight compared with the more boisterous efforts coming from the Lennon and Harrison camps. The John Lennon/Plastic Ono Band disc had been released during December, 1970. Lennon explored his childhood, mother-relationship, adolescent rejection, even Beatle agonies. In

George Harrison devoted himself more and more to his interest in Eastern music and religion, forming a close friendship with Indian sitar virtuoso Ravi Shankar. In 1971 he was the moving spirit behind the huge Concerts for Bangladesh at Madison Square Garden. His love of oriental mysticism found expression in his triple album, **All Things Must Pass.** Meanwhile, the McCartneys' first child, Mary, was born. While all the furore over the Apple empire and Beatles breakup raged, Paul withdrew into the close family life which he has led ever since.

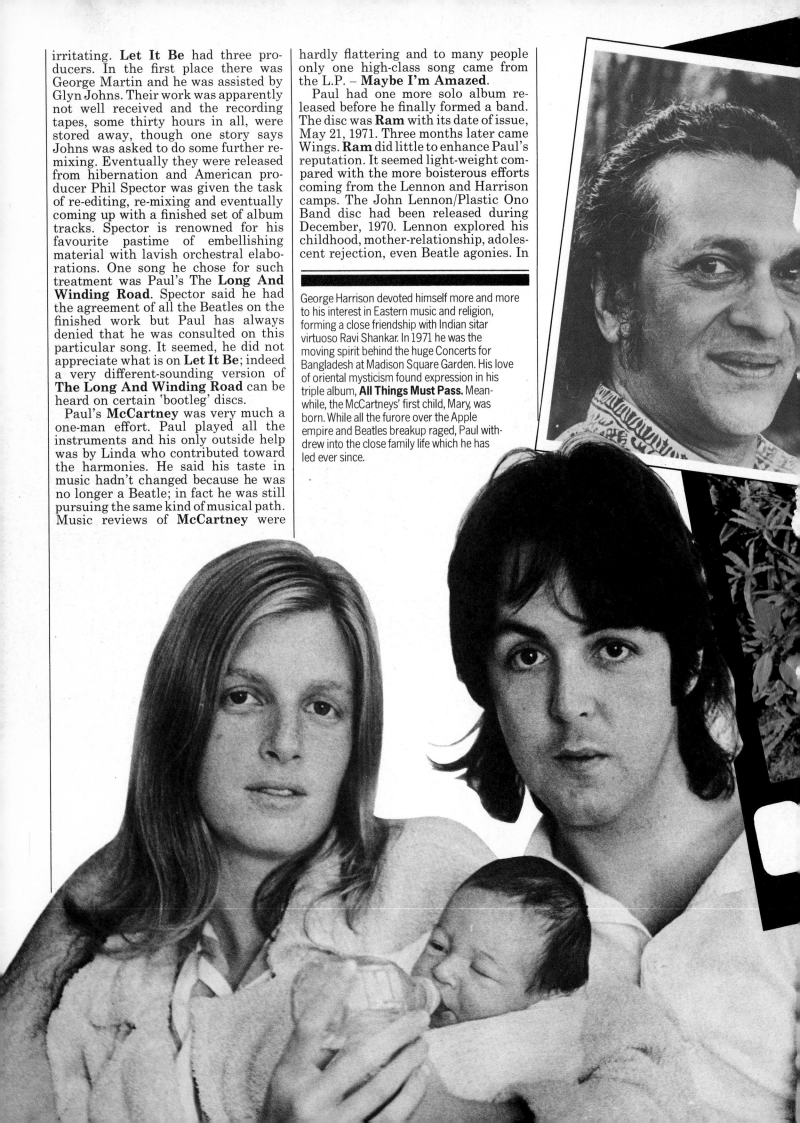

lesser hands it could have been a disaster; as it happened, it succeeded. George Harrison had released **All Things Must Pass**. It gave George's view of the cosmic all and sold heavily. Harrison's spiritual search fitted the times well, for the late 1960s and early '70s was the period when mysticism and Eastern religions were in vogue. It seemed very much 'in' that a leading rock musician should be part of it.

The summer of 1971 saw Harrison concerned with the human problems arising from the war in Bangla Desh and he was very much involved with two concerts held in New York's Madison Square Garden for the purpose of raising money to alleviate the suffering caused by this political turmoil. Eric Clapton, Ringo, Bob Dylan, Leon Russell, Billy Preston and Ravi Shankar were some of the other people involved. George was very much part of rock's hierarchy and was often seen and heard in interview.

Before Wings was born, John had another album released. This was **Imagine** and for some it stands as the best disc which Lennon has made outside of his once-rich partnership with Paul McCartney. Immediate impressions suggested a melodic, flowing album but lurking beneath the outward veneer of pleasantness lay an attack on Paul. The track was **How Do You Sleep**. George played on this particular song and it made the lyric's insults all the more direct. Not content with one swipe at Paul, John Lennon had himself pictured fondling a pig in similar manner to Paul's gesture on the front cover of **Ram** and the picture was enclosed with the album package.

Obviously, if Paul felt his place was in Scotland or whatever, then it was his choice, but when his life-style was placed alongside that of the other Beatles he seemed to be heading for obscurity. It would not have been so bad if **Ram** had suggested that Paul's comparative isolation from the rock world had released a flood of ideas. **Ram**, however, was badly received. People said Paul used every recording trick possible so as to convince people there was a full sound on disc. He was heavily criticized for his extended endings to many songs. Roy Carr and Tony Tyler in their *The Beatles – Illustrated* (New English Library, 1975) expressed the general dissatisfaction with Ram by somewhat caustically writing, 'It was sta-prest ready-to-wear music, to be listened to in a lounge with plaster ducks on the wall. . . . Paul's long-drawn-out yearnings for cucumber sandwiches at the local Rotary Club and a family of his own were further emphasized by the cover photo, taken on his Scottish farm, showing the genial Beatle, gumbooted, fondling a ram.'

But at least Paul had one satisfaction. Both **McCartney** and **Ram** albums made the top two positions both sides of the Atlantic. And in the singles market, Paul also achieved good results. **Another Day**, listed as being written by both Paul and Linda, reached number two in the British charts and five in the States. **Uncle Albert – Admiral Halsey**, from the **Ram** album, was the Stateside follow-up and hit the chart top. Paul McCartney might not have been the rock world's darling at this time but the record-buying public appreciated him.

Outside of Paul's recordings and the activities of the other Beatles, during the period 1970–1, one other strange and newsworthy event caught some people's attention. This was Paul's supposed death. It originated from an American student's term paper. His college journal ran his deductions and in no time the world media ran the story. It went like this: the suggestion was of an imposter playing the role of Paul. Paul had died in 1966! Radio stations in America said Paul had been killed in a car accident. The driver had been young and dark-haired and totally disfigured. No identification had been made. Somehow the deduction was made that this must have been Paul! There were even stories of a Paul look-a-like competition from which someone called William Campbell had been selected. The student concerned for the beginnings of this strange and odd saga had developed an elaborate case from readings made of various Beatle albums. So for instance great attention had been paid to a line in the **Sergeant Pepper** track, **A Day In The Life** which went, 'He blew his mind out in a car' and amazingly it was suggested that if someone played the siren which closes **Strawberry Fields Forever**, at a speed of 16 rpm, then the siren becomes a voice and the words, 'I buried Paul' can be made out. When **Revolution Nine** was played backwards then the words, 'Turn me

on, dead man, turn me on, dead man' could be heard.

Various Beatle album covers also revealed apparently positive clues in nailing fairly and squarely as fact, Paul's death. One piece of evidence from the **Sergeant Pepper** album lay in the letters on Paul's uniform sleeve which read OPD – Officially Pronounced Dead. And then again, on the back cover, who should be the one Beatle with his back turned? – Paul. On the **Magical Mystery Tour** L.P. Paul is the black Walrus while the **White Album** photo strip has one picture of Paul sitting down with crossed flags above him. There in front of him can be seen the words, 'I Was'. If the mind boggled at some of these descriptions, then even more mind-blowing is the evidence deduced from a Volkswagen car seen in the picture of Abbey Road from the album of the same name. The car had a number-plate reading 28IF. Beatle Paul's death investigators assumed this must mean Paul would have been 28 IF he was still alive but then he would have been 27 in 1969. However, someone realized that in the East people believe that everyone is a year old at birth. So Paul would have been 28 and after all, the Beatles had taken great interest in oriental reli-

gions. Paul, at first, found the stories amusing but he soon changed his mind when the media moved in on his Scottish home and interrupted his private life. From the vantage point of time he finds the whole episode one of those things he can now laugh about.

John Lennon's, **Imagine** album, had been released at the beginning of October, 1971. A month later came the first Wings album, **Wild Life**, produced by Paul and Linda. A recording and permanent road band was formed. At the time it seemed odd that Paul should do this. Although he had been the most enthusiastic of the protagonist Beatles for live gigging, only a year before he had proclaimed the benefits of being 'at home' and the joys of being a solo performer who could do what he wanted without the demands and responsibilities of working with a group. Obviously Paul McCartney's love of an audience and of being in a band hadn't died, even if he had enjoyed his solo years. He saw that he could, if he was careful, have the best of both worlds. A successful band could tour for six months of a year and the remainder could be spent as he wished with his family, either at his London or Scottish residences. And so just before the release of **Wings – Wild Life**, the band was introduced to the public. A public relations campaign brought before the world the band's line-up of Paul and Linda, U.S. drummer Denny Seiwell and the ex-Moody Blues vocalist and guitarist, Denny Laine. At that time the group was known as Paul McCartney and

Teaming up with his old friend Denny Laine and drummer Denny Seiwell, McCartney formed his own band, Wings. Once again, the first album, **Wings Wild Life,** had a cool reception from the press, but when Wings went out on the road the fans flocked to see them. This was to be the pattern until **Band On The Run** finally achieved critical acclaim. Although he wanted Wings to be seen as a band in its own right, Paul was still the magnet that drew crowds.

Wings. Paul explained his motives. He said that he had never ruled out forming a band of his own, and that when John Lennon had got together The Plastic Ono Band a similar idea had been revolving in his head. He also spoke about his need to be in front of an audience, hearing the applause and knowing that he was entertaining people.

The album was issued amid another wave of publicity but many found the fanfares a little premature. In their minds, Paul and Wings hadn't yet proved themselves. Much of the musical press hammered the disc and people talked of how low Paul McCartney's credibility could sink before he reached rock bottom. Perhaps there was more than purely musical considerations affecting some critics and their reaction. Maybe it was the case of Paul the unforgiven who, for the moment, could do no right. People who had regarded him as a musical genius with the Beatles now saw him as very ordinary indeed. The general public in Britain and America did not feel quite the same, though the album was by no means the success of Paul's previous two solo outings. It made – but only just – the top ten listings of both countries.

Paul stated his case quite clearly, 'I don't care if people don't like it . . . I like it. I've got an awful lot to live up to, that's the problem. But I know I'm good. If I'm in the right mood I can write a solid gold hit.' He said criticism of **McCartney** had needled him a little and when he had made **Ram** he was conscious of trying to please himself and the critics, not that the latter had shown too much appreciation.

The name Wings for his first live band since the Beatles had come to Paul when Linda was expecting Stella in London's Kings College Hospital. When Mary had been born Paul had been present at the birth but this time a Caesarean operation was needed, and he had to sit and wait in an adjoining room. He went through bouts of nerves and prayed like mad and as Linda told journalist Hunter Davies, 'Wings of an angel, that's what I was thinking about.'

Stella was born without complications, unlike the band's first album. Paul, however, had plans for ensuring that the live band wouldn't be hammered by the press. Wings would hire a special bus and would just drop in at British universities and play. This would give them basic experience as a live band. They would then play some selected European dates before thinking of Britain and eventually the toughest of them all – America.

Wings would take a percentage of the door-money and, for the first time in years, Paul would actually be paid in real live cash. More important, though, these gigs could prove the morale booster Paul needed, the knowledge that people 'out there' did have affection for this ex-Beatle. However, even the immediate rapture the band was to receive from predominantly late-teen, early-twenties audiences, welcome as it was, did not hide from Paul or anyone that the road ahead would be long and the journey tough.

2
THE STORY OF
WINGS

It should have been the ordinary weekly dance at Britain's Nottingham University. When the students turned up, however, they could scarcely believe the hurriedly-written poster that confronted them: 'Tonight! Guest Group – Paul McCartney and Wings! Admission 50p.' For less than a dollar, students had the opportunity of hearing the ex-Beatle and his new band. Such

events do not occur every day, so why this and a number of similar occasions which followed?

Paul has always adored playing before an audience. He, of all the Beatles, was the one who constantly tried to get them back on the road, once they had ceased touring in August 1966, following the American tour which had begun in Chicago and ended in San Francisco.

He formed the group to play live and the last thing he wanted was a studio band who only came together for recordings. At his press conference in November of 1971, when **Wings – Wild Life** was launched, Paul McCartney talked quite freely about his desire for the band to suddenly get up, get into a van and quite simply take off. The band would find some unannounced venues and

just set up and play. This they did for Nottingham and other British university and college students.

Wings began informally and on a casual basis without trumpeting and clarion cries, although this contrasted strongly with the fanfares which were blown over the band's first and not-too-well-received album. Why, though, the secrecy? It seemed Paul felt that any official announcement would lead to an enormous flow of media attention and scores of letters for tickets flooding someone's office desk. The group would find themselves forced into playing at large halls. Once that happened, then the whole press and media would be there, busily writing their reviews and comments, and Paul did not want this kind of situation for the band in its

Wings–first edition–included guitarist Henry McCullough and drummer Denny Seiwell, together with the faithful Denny Laine and, of course, Linda on keyboards.

infancy. He himself did not want the personal strain of first night nerves, as, for instance, seen in the emotional turmoil John Lennon had gone through

1972. Wings – still with McCullough – embarked on their first European tour. They announced that they would all travel in an open-top double decker bus. Although they had pictures taken aboard, and it trundled dutifully around with them, the bus was not used very much for actual touring journeys. The trip lasted seven weeks and took in 26 cities. They were arrested in Stockholm for smoking cannabis and fined by the authorities.

when he was due to appear at the Toronto Peace Rally. Those close to Paul knew he had no wish to expose Linda to hard critics. It was his personal choosing that his wife, a non-musician and inexperienced stage performer, should be fully part of his new musical life since his declaration of independence from the Beatles. She needed time. And indeed at one gig, at Leeds University, Linda was suddenly overcome with nerves as the band rolled into the opening chords of **Wild Life**. Fortunately the audience thought it part of the act as Paul went over and gave his wife the necessary encouragement. So the story of Wings, after the publicity of their first album, began at leisurely pace. The band's gigging before audiences who were grateful for a cheap evening of fine music was an ideal way of picking up confidence. Eventually, of course, the band began playing small tours in Europe, but not before spending happy days touring up and down Britain. In one or two instances there were some headaches, as on the occasion when they arrived in one town only to find that it did not have a college or university, and in another the students were busily sitting exams.

Controversy was not far away. Early in 1972, Paul became involved with the political problems of Northern Ireland and why, it might be asked, should Paul have suddenly become taken up with front-page newspaper events, in the

manner more associated with John Lennon? Paul is of course from Liverpool and a large part of that city's population is of Irish descent. Indeed, the city is often jokingly referred to as the 'capital of Ireland'. The McCartneys, as their name suggests, are Liverpool-Irish and proud of it. And this may well explain why Paul decided to record, under the Wings imprint, the first and only propaganda song he has ever written. **Give Ireland Back To The Irish** was his instinctive emotional reaction to the strife in Northern Ireland. The disc was not played by Britain's only national pop radio station, BBC Radio One. At the same time the station refused to play **Let the People Go** from McGuinness Flint. The reason for both discs not gaining airplay was, according to the BBC Press

Officer, Rodney Collins, because the discs made a political point, rather than merely saying there was a great deal of sadness and suffering arising from the political mess. The BBC is, of course, not an independent commercial station and has responsibilities which are not necessarily those of companies whose revenue does not come from a national, compulsory licence system.

Paul's disc was entirely sympathetic to the Catholic cause and in its lyrics it was as heavy as anything John Lennon had ever put on disc. Paul said he was saddened by the Irish situation; he felt once it was the Protestants against Catholics, whereas now it was the Irish against the English. One or two music critics, without questioning Paul's integrity, did worry over how some people would receive the disc, particularly

Wings established themselves as a working band and appeared on the BBC show **Top Of The Pops.** Meanwhile, Ringo Starr revealed hitherto unsuspected talents as a movie actor in **That'll Be The Day,** in which he played a greasy fairground worker and practically stole the show from David Essex. He also appeared in **The Magic Christian** with Peter Sellars. Ringo was turning out to be a show business celebrity in his own right; he even shaved his hair off at one point. The other Beatles continued with their lives as before. John Lennon managed to hang on in the States, battling the immigration authorities and working with Yoko on recording projects.

the men and women of violence. But the critics were, in the main, agreed on one thing; from a purely pop music standpoint the disc had a lot going for

it. New member of then three weeks, Henry McCullough, played slide guitar, Paul sang and gave a rather severe wailing sound to some lines he thought particularly expressive of suffering and Linda provided electric piano backing. The record did enter the charts but never became a major chart hit in Britain. It entered the Top 20 on March 11 and reached a highest position of 16.

Three months later came another chart single. **Mary Had A Little Lamb** did reach the Top 10, though it was hardly loved by music reviewers. In Roy Carr and Tony Tyler's volume, *The Beatles – An Illustrated Record* the disc is described as a deplorable single. The writers comment, 'It is difficult not to draw the conclusion that McCartney, piqued at the banning of his **Give Ireland Back To The Irish** single, deliberately recorded nursery lyrics as

a gesture of contempt towards the censors in question.' Paul told Paul Gambaccini that he had always thought John crackers for singing all his political songs and that he himself had never thought it a particular avenue of expression he would bring himself to consider. Then, he changed his mind. When Gambaccini asked him about **Mary Had A Little Lamb**, Paul appeared to hedge the question and merely remarked that the song was a nursery rhyme and he thought it would be pleasant for everyone to find out what the original words were.

While Paul involved Wings with the Irish question, Ringo was busily working, in part with George Harrison, on Ringo's single, **Back Off Boogaloo**. He had also become a film-maker.

On July 9, 1972 Wings decided to venture forth into the bigger arena of

the European audience. On that date, they played at the Château Fallon, France but in August some of Paul's cosy image disappeared when he and Linda were arrested by the Swedish authorities for drug possession. It seemed a strange affair but it did appear that someone had tapped the McCartney phones, had heard that a small order of marijuana from Britain was expected, and this was impounded on its arrival. However, eventually things were sorted out. In Sweden, it seems, Paul's lyrics are utilized for teaching Swedish young people English.

Another drug bust was to follow a month later at the McCartney Scottish home and this time the authorities found some marijuana plants. It all seemed for a moment as if the drug raids of the Stones era in the 1960s were going to be repeated, with Paul this time the

The BBC TV show **James Paul McCartney** presented him in a variety of roles, including a pub sing-song and an Astaire-type chorus number. It was a good reflection of his very broad tastes in pop music styles. Linda doubled as Wings-member and resident photographer. The show was Paul's idea. He is very keen on the visual presentation of his music and it is strange that he does so little television work.

sacrificial victim, so that wayward youth could be taught a lesson. Fortunately, this didn't happen.

Sandwiched in between Paul's drug busts, John Lennon had, on August 30, been part of a star billing which sang and played for two charity shows at New York's Madison Square Garden to help handicapped children. And four days before Paul's Scottish bust on

September 20, 1972, Lennon, with the Plastic Ono Band, released **Some Time In New York City**, with the Frank Zappa band playing on some tracks. In November, Lennon with the Children's Choir of Harlem Community Centre, issued the splendid Christmas song, **Happy Xmas War Is Over**. Paul and Wings seemed in less concilliatory mood for the festive season. Wings released **Hi Hi Hi** with **C Moon** on the B-side. The BBC did not play the A-side, though it reached number five, entering the charts on January 3, 1973, a month or so after its release. In America the disc reached 10, but spent just over a month in the Top 20, so it was hardly a success compared with later records like **Band On The Run**

and **Let 'Em In**. The reason for **Hi Hi Hi** being banned lay in its suspected advocacy of drugs. Radio One concentrated on **C Moon** instead, and some felt it was not an unwise decision, since **C Moon**, with its reggae flavour, was the better of the two sides from a composition point of view.

Paul's view on the lyric of **Hi Hi Hi** was simple, it could be taken as a reference to any kind of high, which might, for instance, come from alcohol. However, as Paul told Paul Gambaccini, matters were not helped by a somewhat amusing mistake – although it wasn't funny at the time, when emotions on all sides of the fence were flying high. Paul noticed the lyrics supplied by Northern Songs, the publishing company contained the extraordinary line, 'Get ready for my body gun' which, Paul said, sounded much more suggestive than 'Get ready for my polygon, watch out baby', which he had actually

sung on the record. 1973 was a mixture of good and bad and, in general ex-Beatle terms, quite tempestuous. For John Lennon there were marital difficulties and a further crucial stage in his eventually long-standing battle with the U.S. Immigration Authorities. In March of '73 he was ordered to leave the States. In his usual colourful fashion he informed the authorities that he and Yoko were not prepared to sleep in separate beds.

In May, EMI in Britain and Capitol, U.S.A. issued two double albums of big Beatle numbers from the periods, 1962–66 and 1967–70 and a mild epidemic of Beatlemania broke out. Wings were busy at the time, working on the album, **Red Rose Speedway** in May. Previously there had been a single issued from the album, **My Love**. It

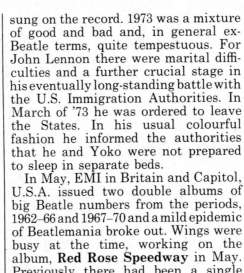

was one of those sentimental ballads with which Paul either delights or infuriates the listener. The single was issued in March, the same month in which McCartney was yet again busted for drugs, this time for growing five cannabis plants. Some people once more suspected that there was deliberate intent to make an example of Paul. It was, perhaps, this further bust which prompted him into playing a benefit concert for 'Release', a British organization devoted to helping people with drug problems. As someone cynically remarked, his succession of drug busts did his reputation no end of good in the more heavy rock scene.

In April, 1973, Paul talked of a possible Beatle reunion, quite a contrast from a previous month's statement from Ringo that such a development

was not possible. One could only hazard a guess at how he reacted toward the announcement that the other three Beatles were no longer in contract with Allan Klein and what he thought of Klein's action in actually suing John Lennon. He, McCartney, appeared to have been in the right all along.

The first half of 1973 also saw Paul writing the theme song for the James Bond movie, **Live And Let Die**. It gave the film a fillip and at the same time it became a UK Top 10 single. The disc reached number two in America. It has, in time, become one of the most popular numbers in the band's repertoire. McCartney wrote a fine tune and the disc, which includes some rather eerie vocals from Linda and Denny, deservedly won its acclaim. In fact, McCartney was revving up toward a

hit run starting with the single of **Helen Wheels**. Wings were, at long last, on their first British tour, which had commenced during the Spring. Just before this tour, there was a press-preview of the forthcoming television film, **James Paul McCartney**. It was transmitted in June. It showed Paul's Merseyside home territory and some familiar pop figures from the early 1960s, including Gerry Marsden, of Gerry And The Pacemakers who had several British and U.S. hits during Beatlemania days. There was a British pub sing-a-long too and Paul, with slicked-down hair, tails and golden shoes did a little dance routine. In contrast, there was an all-action clip of the James Bond film, to go with Paul's theme tune. The T.V. film contained a Beatle medley and, just when

Band On The Run was recorded by Paul, Linda and Denny Laine in Lagos, Nigeria. McCullough and Seiwell left the group on the eve of departure. They were replaced by Geoff Britton and Jimmy McCulloch. Britton was chosen at an audition, but did not remain with Wings for very long.

some people must have wondered 'when', there came a tight and engaging set from Wings themselves. The film ended with Paul singing **Yesterday**.

The Spring 1973 British tour was a success. By the end of each concert bouncers and roadies had to prevent the surge of enthusiastic people from climbing onto the stage. Wings were very much what they had promised, a good tight rock 'n' roll band with an act which was beautifully paced. Among

the featured songs were **Seaside Woman, Live And Let Die, Wild Life, Say You Don't Mind, Maybe I'm Amazed, My Love, Hi Hi Hi, The Mess I'm In** and **Go Now**. The encore was the song which had made Little Richard, among others, popular back in the first rock 'n' roll era, **Long Tall Sally**.

At the end of the tour Paul spoke again with the press. He said there had been some dodgy moments but, at least in the beginning, they had been able to pretend in some degree that they were a small time group. He was asked whether there had been a point when he felt it just wouldn't work out. Paul replied, 'Once or twice, you know we had a few kinda arguments and stuff like "I don't like the way you do that" and . . . oogh, friction.' Paul was asked whether it was he who made the decisions. Wings was described as a democratic band, but Paul said that, if there had to be a definite decision, then he made it. He spoke of letting Denny Laine have more of a central part in the stage act. Inevitably, someone asked him about the Beatles and he partly parried by talking of how he enjoyed something new and for him this was Wings. He enjoyed the live audience, particularly their reaction to good, lively, rocking numbers. What was important, he thought, was being aware of the times. He said, 'You could develop the most incredible Beatle or McCartney act and blow it by not keeping up with the times. Then it's going to be "Oh they're a very nice nostalgic group" and I don't want that.' As for America, it was out of the question because of Paul's drug offences; he had no U.S. visa. And then, quite unexpectedly, two members of Wings quit – Denny Seiwell and Henry McCullough. Seiwell's departure was particularly surprising, since he had spoken in interviews of his enthusiasm for the band and their plans for the future. McCullough made no secret of the cause of his discontent; it was Linda. 'I wouldn't have Linda in a band,' he told the *Melody Maker* in 1977. 'She doesn't have a musical head on her.'

McCullough left on August 25 and

prevented him getting together with them. He thought that there could now be a Beatle reunion.

It was not to be so, though intense pressure for the group's re-forming proceeded unabated, with a peak point during early autumn of 1974.

Helen Wheels was issued on October 20 with **Country Dreamer** as the B-side. It was a great choice, for critics began writing of the long-expected post-Beatle McCartney flowering at last taking place. Interesting also was the day's other event, the release of Ringo's **Photograph.**

In December, and at long last, Paul obtained his American visa and the way was open for Wings to make an American tour. There was another Christmas present for McCartney. On December 22, **Helen Wheels** entered the Billboard Top 20.

However, what made the McCartney's Christmas, more than anything, were the generally rave reviews for **Band**

Wings were jubilant over the success of **Band On The Run.** Paul, Linda and Denny had quite a collection of gold discs by now, both for this album and its predecessor, **Red Rose Speedway.** Perhaps for the first time everything was going fine, with chart-topping singles and a world-wide album hit. In the same month – December 1973 – Ringo's LP is released, with one track, **Six O'Clock,** written by Paul.

On The Run. And from it came two big chart singles, **Jet** and the title-track, **Band On The Run**. The album showed McCartney bringing together all the things he excels at, lots of melody, good, tight, driving arrangements and an air of great confidence pervading the whole thing. For most people, McCartney's future looked great, if only he could find a drummer and guitarist who would stay. **Jet** was in the British and American Top 20 listings in March and **Band On The Run** in the U.S. May charts. Its release was delayed in Britain and there it was a summer smash, though it only made number three, compared with being a chart topper in the States.

Beatle get-together chatter continued while **Band On The Run** flourished, in part due to Wings still not yet being a stable playing unit. And John Lennon was in the throes of more tempestous days. He had talked of a Beatle get-together as possible and if so, it would be a wonderful event. Paul agreed they could be working together, though not necessarily under the Beatle name. Lennon meantime became more pre-occupied with his problem of not being

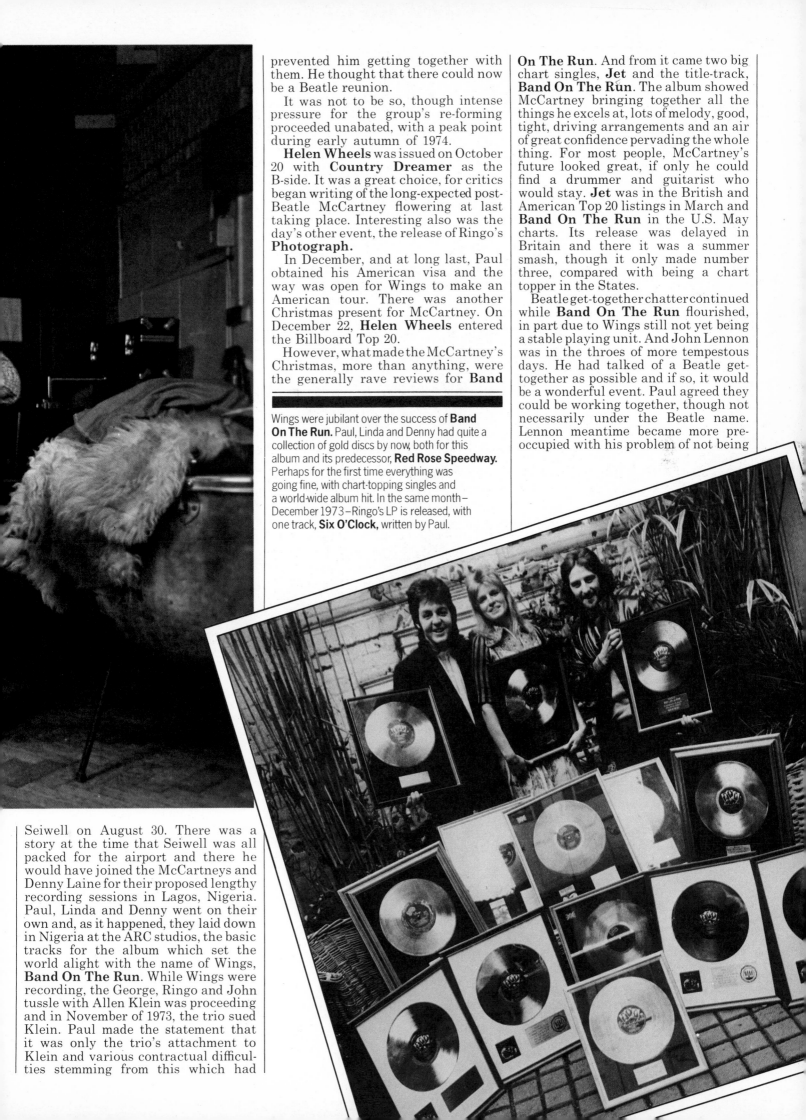

Seiwell on August 30. There was a story at the time that Seiwell was all packed for the airport and there he would have joined the McCartneys and Denny Laine for their proposed lengthy recording sessions in Lagos, Nigeria. Paul, Linda and Denny went on their own and, as it happened, they laid down in Nigeria at the ARC studios, the basic tracks for the album which set the world alight with the name of Wings, **Band On The Run**. While Wings were recording, the George, Ringo and John tussle with Allen Klein was proceeding and in November of 1973, the trio sued Klein. Paul made the statement that it was only the trio's attachment to Klein and various contractual difficulties stemming from this which had able to leave the United States since, if he did, he would be refused re-entry, owing to his past drug conviction. He even petitioned the Queen for pardon. By February, so the press reported, he was on the verge of splitting from Yoko and more drama came when, in March, he was thrown out of a famous Los Angeles club, The Troubadour, for insulting the Smothers Brothers and assaulting the manager and a waitress.

George Harrison was also busy and he formed his own record company, Dark Horse, in June of '74. Meantime, Paul had been recording in Nashville and there he, Linda and Denny were joined by their new guitarist, Jimmy McCulloch. Geoff Britton became the band's drummer, though not for long, in spite of his initial enthusiasm.

Nashville meant the recording of **Junior's Farm**, a rocker if ever there was one, and it had some critics considering that perhaps McCartney had at last ceased being a Beatle. Some even went further and wrote that McCartney had found a new band. Whatever the case, McCartney must have been pleased. **Junior's Farm** had British release in October, but before its issue there was news of another McCartney project, this time with his brother Mike McGear.

McGear had found British fame with a group called Scaffold, who had two Top 20 hits during the 1967–8 period, **Thank U Very Much** and **Lily The Pink**. They were very much a sophisticated style comedy group in their live performances, while on disc they performed rather down-market comedy material, especially popular with children. Scaffold, save for select occasions, more or less ceased operation during the early '70s though McGear, with his singing and poetry, had carried on performing and had appeared on several television programmes. He also had ideas of putting together a solo album.

The two brothers, Paul and Mike, had kept apart over the years, as far as recording was concerned, but now they had decided the time was ripe for working together.

The two present quite a contrast. Mike, on first impression, bears little resemblance to Paul, in physical appearance and his personality is quite different.

Paul is a quiet person, until he becomes excited about something, whereas Mike seems far more of an extrovert. McGear is one of those people forever bounding forward from a hunched-sitting position: his hands are used to emphasise a point and the face, more often than not, wears a smile.

Mike's recording, with Paul as producer, had a spin-off, for Paul had a composition called **Liverpool Lou**. He thought it would be a good number for the defunct Scaffold. Scaffold (Mike, Roger McGough and John Gorman) got together and recorded the McCartney song, and found themselves with a hit. The record entered the Top 20 on

June 15 and it reached number seven. As with former hits, **Thank U Very Much** and **Lily The Pink**, there was no corresponding US Top 20 entry.

US Beatlemania reached another peak as July 1974 drew to its close, with the first-ever Boston Beatle Convention, followed a few months later by one organized by Sid Bernstein. Bernstein had promoted the Beatles back in the 1960s, for their Shea stadium gig. In 1975 he became heavily involved with the Bay City Rollers and became their American manager. For Beatlefest '74, 4000 people packed the ballroom of New York's Hotel Commodore. It was an occasion for non-stop talk, films, exhibitions, and music, auctions of valued Beatle momentos and a raffle which raised almost $3,000 for a New York self-help drug programme. For the raffle, the prize offered was the tabla George played on **Sgt Pepper**, autographed Ringo drumsticks, and guitars from both John and Paul. T-shirts were sold and according to the sellers, official and unofficial, the Beatle who sold best was Paul of Wings.

The Beatle conventions sparked off further talk of Beatle re-union, or at least promoters waxed eloquent on the money which might be made.

Naturally, everyone would get their appropriate split of the proceeds. The kind of project envisaged went far beyond just an actual concert, for that would form the base of a massive money-making bonanza. The concert would be sold to T.V. and films and, if it were beamed live to stadiums or halls throughout the world, takings would be enormous. There would be a radio special and perhaps a major sponsor would put money into it for the reward of world advertising rights. There would, of course, be all the eventual spin-offs of souvenirs, toys, T-shirts, posters, programmes, books and booklets and even Beatle lunchboxes, key chains, notebooks. Who could say where it might all end! One conserservative estimate thought there might be $50 million at least for distribution. One American promoter Jerry Perenchio could see the event making $100 million gross if done for charity and, as far as he was concerned, 'they could do it in my living room, if that's what they wanted.'

But they didn't. Paul was getting more and more involved with Wings and John Lennon had been ordered out of the States by The Board of Immigration Appeals. Meantime, in Britain, there were packed houses for a more adult form of Beatle worship, as the show, **John, Paul, George, Ringo . . . and Bert** opened. This musical, which traced some of the Fab Four's story in words and their songs, eventually made New York in December, of 1974. There

The brothers. Paul produced Mike's solo album, **McGear,** and Wings played the backing tracks. They had a British hit single with **Liverpool Lou.**

it joined the musical of **Sergeant Pepper's Lonely Hearts Club Band**, which had already made itself at home in the Beacon theatre.

In real life, Ringo was having marital problems and George Harrison announced his days with Patti Boyd were over. Meanwhile, Paul continued hand-in-hand with Linda as Wings stormed the American charts during November with **Junior's Farm** and settled for a top placing at three, plus two months or so in the Top 20. Oddly enough, though many British critics raved over the disc in the United Kingdom, there was but a solitary week's Top 20 outing, at 16. It was a mystery, particularly in view of previous chart successes, **Band On The Run, Jet** and **Helen Wheels.**

By the end of 1974, **Band On The Run** had sold over six million copies in album form and it had achieved the unique feat of making the US *Billboard* magazine's album Hot 200, at number one, on three separate occasions.

In 1975 came another hit album, **Venus and Mars.** From this album came two singles, **Listen To What The Man Said** and a remix for single form of **Letting Go.** Joe English became a member of Wings in 1975 and the band finally settled down with a stable personnel. This was the band which would record **Wings At The Speed of Sound** and tour the world, starting in Southampton in the autumn They would play concerts in Australia, Denmark Austria, Holland, Germany, Italy, Canada, Yugoslavia and the USA.

One of Britain's more earthy Sunday newspapers, *The People*, ran the McCartney Family as a story. It seemed so unusual to their reporter that anyone at the top of the pop world could actually lead a normal, stable family existence. Paul did say he was no longer the swinging bachelor of the 1960s.

Paul finally severed the Apple label imprint from Wings' releases in 1975 and instead Wings returned to the old Capitol logo of the 1950s. In Britain, all Wings and other ex-Apples are still officially on Parlophone, the Beatles' old label.

Surprisingly, the two singles did rather poorly but Wings were too active and too successful to be affected. There would be no point in any music journalist writing a story on the lines that Wings were grinding to a halt, just at the point where they had seemingly taken off in a major way.

The tour which took Wings from September of 1975 to late-autumn, 1976 was a tremendous success, though it was not without incident and even a slight degree of unpleasantness. The less welcome side involved the group's proposed gigs in Japan. Visas were signed by the Japanese Embassy and ace photographer David Bailey was flying in to make a film of the Wings visit. Then, suddenly, the Japanese Minister of Justice said they could not come because of Paul's record of convictions for drug offences. He was

upset and disappointed. He commented on one occasion, 'I suppose he'd say it was my fault for having smoked some of the deadly weed.' As it happened, Wings, who were in Australia during the final movement of this affair, made a television film of their act for Australians who could not get to their concerts. The film was dispatched to Japan where, to Paul's surprise, on the weekend the band should have been in Japan, a ninety minute debate took place on the marijuana question.

The major tour incident, apart from this somewhat unpleasant episode took place after the group's Paris concert in

The McCartneys are not great party-goers, but they often attend concerts by other rock stars. One such occasion was the Faces' London show during their Christmas tour of 1974. Rod Stewart is a champion horrible-face puller.

1976. They were being taken from the theatre in a cavalcade of cars. The fast-moving procession suddenly stopped with a screeching of brakes and guitarist, Jimmy McCulloch was thrown forward and, in falling, broke a finger of his left hand. This meant that he would be unable to play for several weeks and, in consequence, the eagerly-awaited American tour had to be postponed. It was too late however, printing schedules being what they are, to stop Britain's *Sunday Times* publishing, in their issue of April 4, a long article on the forthcoming American visit. Apart from their touring, 1976 was marked by the release of **Wings At The Speed**

Of Sound with its two successful singles, **Let 'Em In** and **Silly Love Songs** and the eventual **Wings Over America.** The latter must rank as one of the finest 'live' albums ever. In Beatle territory, John Lennon had received permission to come and go from America as he pleased. George Harrison was in court for a decision over whether his famous number one hit, **My Sweet Lord** was a blatant copy of the old pop number, **He's So Fine.** Harrison lost the case but expressed his pleasure at being free of worries and consequently able to devote more time toward recordings. During the Christmas season his disc entitled **Thirty**

Three and One-Third was issued. The title was a reference to his age at the time of recording. Most critics agreed it was Harrison's best for some time, after several rather poor discs.

Lennon, though, remained silent as far as recordings were concerned. In Britain, at Christmas, there was a slight push once more behind his previous Christmas hit single, **Happy**

Xmas War Is Over. If Lennon was silent, so too was Ringo.

McCartney was plagued throughout 1976 with questions about Beatle comebacks, helped by the revival of Beatle singles popularity on both sides of the Atlantic. At one time, it did seem possible that all the British Top 20 would comprise Beatle discs. For the first time in Britain Paul's **Yesterday** was issued as a single; formerly it had been part of an Extended Play disc, unlike in the States, where it had been a single and a number one during the winter of 1965. Paul commented favourably on its release, and the general reaction to all the old Beatle singles

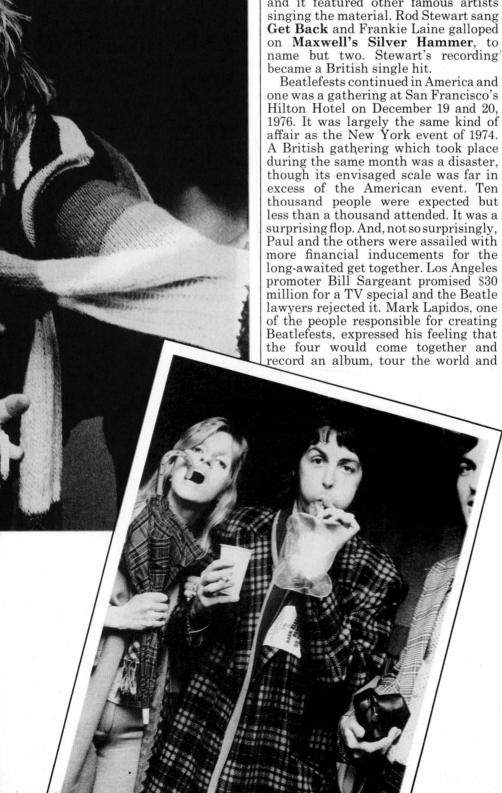

gave him the thrill of knowing another generation adored the music he and the other three had made.

Both the American and British record companies owning Beatle material raided previous album material for fresh singles and a compilation of mostly rock 'n' roll material was issued in album form under the title of **Rock 'n' Roll Music**, while **Sgt Pepper** kept coming in and out of the album listings in Britain and the States.

A **'Best of George Harrison'** was issued. This travelled back to Beatle album days and naturally included the early solo material made before Harrison formed his own company. A film of Beatle songs was made under the title of **All This and World War II** and it featured other famous artists singing the material. Rod Stewart sang **Get Back** and Frankie Laine galloped on **Maxwell's Silver Hammer**, to name but two. Stewart's recording became a British single hit.

Beatlefests continued in America and one was a gathering at San Francisco's Hilton Hotel on December 19 and 20, 1976. It was largely the same kind of affair as the New York event of 1974. A British gathering which took place during the same month was a disaster, though its envisaged scale was far in excess of the American event. Ten thousand people were expected but less than a thousand attended. It was a surprising flop. And, not so surprisingly, Paul and the others were assailed with more financial inducements for the long-awaited get together. Los Angeles promoter Bill Sargeant promised $30 million for a TV special and the Beatle lawyers rejected it. Mark Lapidos, one of the people responsible for creating Beatlefests, expressed his feeling that the four would come together and record an album, tour the world and

make a worldwide TV special.

American promoter Sid Bernstein scooped everybody for ingenuity by pleading for Beatle reunion in a full-page advert in The *New York Times*, while the New York hip paper, *Village Voice* had an advert from a group of people calling themselves 'The International Committee To Reunite The Beatles' and subtitled 'A By The People For The People Promotion' with the tail-end of the ad reading 'Let's get The Beatles together again, Let It Be.'

The American rock journal, *Creem*, claimed the event would have happened during 1976, if John Lennon's cab driver hadn't lost his way. According to writer, Barry Dillon, the US NBC-TV smash hit T.V. programme, *Saturday Night*, a satirical show in the vein of Rowan and Martin's *Laugh In*, said that for a joke they would pay the Beatles three thousand dollars for being on the show and put them up in a pretty dire New York hotel. Dillon said John and Paul had seen the show. George was a fan of the programme and Ringo was with him when the other two phoned. They all thought it would be a good idea if they rebounded the joke on the programme organizers and turned up. Which they all did, save for John. He couldn't remember the NBC studio address. He turned up late and by then the programme had been off the air for twenty minutes. Beatle drama for real hit the 1977 headlines, for the legal dispute with Allen Klein was settled, with the American manager receiving the sum of £2,941,000. Britain's *Daily Telegraph* for January 12, 1977, quoted EMI as saying there had been nearly 40 Beatle records in the top 100 some weeks during 1976 and that the group had sold 100 million singles and 100 million albums in 220 countries. Their pre-Apple days were thought to have earned them some £15 million gross.

Sid Bernstein made the offer of the century by dangling a possible £260 million before the four and made the bizarre suggestion that the gig could be at Bethlehem or Liverpool.

While all this was going on during 1976, Wings were touring and receiving enormous acclaim. Their touring ended for the time being in October, 1976 but then, of course, came the album, **Wings Over America**. They entered 1977 with a smash hit L.P.

Away from records, McCartney has interested himself in various other projects. His company has, for instance, bought the publishing rights to all the compositions of the late Buddy Holly. They have also acquired the film rights for the vintage British kids' cartoon character, Rupert the Bear.

In fact, film is one of Paul's abiding interests. Beatles fans will remember that he was the leading spirit in the **Magical Mystery Tour** project. There are said to be many hours of film stored away at his headquarters, including scenes shot at recording sessions and on tour.

CALENDAR OF EVENTS

1969

March 12
Paul marries Linda Eastman.

1970

April 10
Paul says he is leaving the Beatles.
April 17
Paul's first solo album, *McCartney* is issued.
May 8
Let It Be from the Beatles is issued. It contains *Two Of Us*, *One After 909* by John and Paul. From Paul, *Let It Be*, *I've Got A Feeling*, *The Long And Winding Road*, *Get Back*.
December 30
Ringo, John, George are sued by Paul.

1971

February 26
British release for *Another Day*
May 21
Ram, Paul's second solo album issued.
August 3
The formation of Wings is announced.
August 14
British release of *The Back Seat Of My Car*, a single.
November 15
The release for *Wild Life*. L.P.

1972

February 9
Wings play Nottingham University, their first live gig.
February 19
Single, *Give Ireland Back To The Irish*, issued.
May 6
British release of single,

Mary Had A Little Lamb.
July 9
Wings commence tour of Europe.
August 10
Swedish authorities accuse McCartneys of drug possession.
September 20
British police raid the McCartneys' Scottish residence.
December 2
British release of *Hi Hi Hi* coupled with *C Moon*, the side played by the B.B.C.

1973

March 9
Paul fined for growing cannabis plants.
March 24
British release of *My Love*.
May 5
L.P. *Red Rose Speedway* issued. It coincides with group's first major U.K. tour.
June 1
Release of *Live And Let Die* and the song is title song of the James Bond movie of same name.
June 7
British TV Special, *James Paul McCartney*.
August 25
Henry McCullough leaves Wings
August 30
Denny Seiwell leaves group. The other three fly off to Nigeria.

October 20
British release of *Helen Wheels*.
December
U.S.A. grant Paul a visa. *Band On The Run*, officially released Britain, January, 1974, available before Christmas.

1974

February 8
Release of *Jet* in U.K. as a single.

Spring
Here or a little later, McCartney and Wings are in Nashville, U.S.A. Jimmy McCulloch joins band, so does Geoff Britton, during the next few months.
June 28
Release of *Band On The Run*, single. Also around this time, Paul records with Mike McGear.
October 26
Junior's Farm is issued in Britain as a single.

1975

May
Venus and Mars L.P. released. Joe English has been recording with band and he replaces a departed Geoff Britton.

September
9 World tour commences at Southampton, Gaumont
10 Bristol Hippodrome
11 Cardiff Capitol
12 Manchester Free Trade Hall
13 Birmingham Hippodrome
15 Liverpool Empire
16 Newcastle City Hall
17 Hammersmith Odeon, London
18 Hammersmith Odeon, London
20 Edinburgh Usher Hall
21 Glasgow Apollo
22 Aberdeen Capitol
23 Dundee Caird Hall

November
1 Perth Entertainment Centre
4/5 Apollo Stadium, Adelaide
7/8 Sydney Hordern Pavilion
10/11 Brisbane Festival Hall
13/14 Melbourne Myer Music Bowl

1976

April
Wings at the Speed of Sound L.P. released.

May
3 Forth Worth, Tarrant County Convention Centre
4 Houston,

The Summit
7/8 Detroit, Olympia Stadium
9 Toronto, Maple Leaf Gardens
10 Detroit, Richfield Coliseum
12 Philadelphia, Spectrum
14 Philadelphia, Spectrum
15/16 Washington, Capital Centre
18/19 Atlanta, The Omni
21 Nassau—Long Island, Coliseum
22 Boston, The Garden
24/25 New York, Madison Square Gardens
27 Cincinatti, River Front Coliseum
29 Kansas City, Kemper Arena
31 Chicago Stadium

June
1/2 Chicago, Stadium
4 St Paul—Minneapolis, Civic Centre Arena
7 Denver, McNichols Arena
10 Seattle, King Dome
13/14 San Francisco, Cow Palace
16 San Diego, The Sports Arena
18 Tucson,

Community Centre
21/ Los Angeles, The
22/23 Forum

September
19 Stadthalle, Vienna, Austria
21 Dom Sportova Hall, Zagreb, Yugoslavia
25 St Mark's Square, Venice, Italy
27 Olympiahalle, Munich, Germany

October
19 Wembley Empire Pool
20 Wembley Empire Pool
21 Wembley Empire Pool

December
Wings Over America is released as a triple album. Paul and Linda attend Rod Stewart's London concert.

1977

February
The single, *Maybe I'm Amazed* is issued in the U.K.
Also during February, a Roy Harper L.P. is issued and on one track, there are backing vocals from Paul, Linda and Denny, who were, it seems, passing by the recording studios. Enjoying Roy's sound, they suggested adding their particular ingredients!

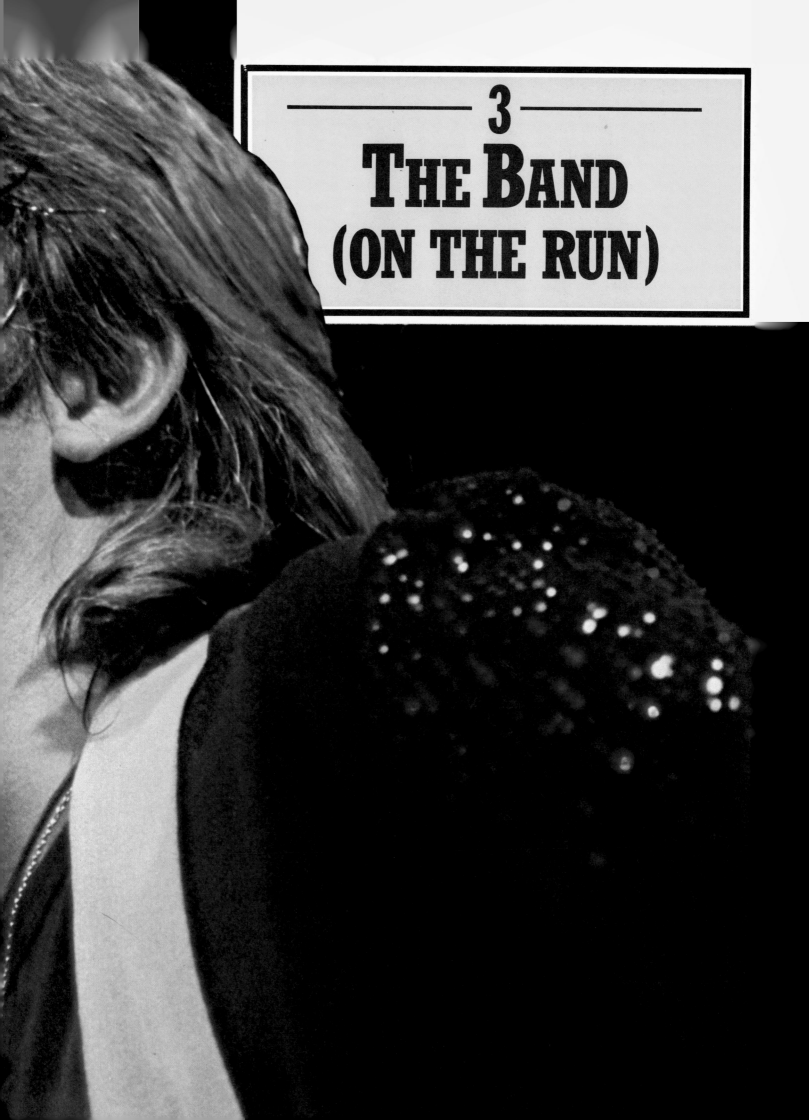

3
THE BAND
(ON THE RUN)

Paul McCartney

They call James Paul McCartney rock's boss bass man but this is only one of the many accolades which could come the way of this talented Englishman from Merseyside's Liverpool. McCartney was a member of pop's greatest ever group, The Beatles, in which he shone as a musician and vocalist. He, with fellow Beatle, John Lennon, formed the most successful song-writing partnership ever seen on the contemporary music scene. Dick James, head of Dick James Music and D.J.M. records, who published all the Beatle songs, has said, 'Together they were as great as Rodgers and Hart'. Their two names also adorn the credits of many records by artists who covered Beatle songs. They also wrote songs for other singers. Examples include Mary Hopkin's, **Goodbye, I Wanna Be Your Man** by The Rolling Stones and Cilla Black's, **Step Inside Love**. Since he began his solo days and as a member of Wings, Paul McCartney has continued with his writing. He has also written for a number of other artists, including Rod Stewart, Ringo Starr and Peggy Lee.

James Paul McCartney was born in Liverpool's Walton Hospital, on June 18, 1942. Both his parents, Jim and Mary Patricia, were of Irish extraction. His mother was once the Sister of the maternity ward in which he was born. In Liverpool, he was reared in a comfortable home and received a good grammar school education.

Paul grew up with music as a common place sound in his home. His dad had been a trumpet player and Paul began his musical path by having trumpet lessons. He didn't carry them to any length but he can still get a tune out of the trumpet. His father at one time ran Jim Mac's Band which, among a number of musical styles, played ragtime. The band played at local functions and it was Paul's dad who bought, for the then not inconsiderable sum of £15, Paul's first guitar. Paul also had piano lessons and for a time he was a member of St. Chad's Church choir.

Paul first heard John at Woolton Parish Church Youth Club. He established immediate contact with this guy who was two years his senior. Both liked the number, **Twenty Flight Rock** and McCartney remembers he knew a few guitar chords Lennon hadn't played. The group he heard Lennon playing in that day was the Quarrymen and he joined its line-up. Later he, with Quarrymen John Lennon and George

The early Beatles–Pete Best, George Harrison, John Lennon, Paul McCartney and Stuart Sutcliffe. They gained their early experience playing in clubs in West Germany, and even made their first records there. But it wasn't until they returned to Liverpool that they met Brian Epstein who was to be their manager and set them on the road to stardom. Their first hit record was **Love Me Do.**

HUGO HAAS
HANNOVER

20 km

Harrison, became part of the Silver Beatles and eventually the Beatles. The Silver Beatles toured Scotland and played a residency in Hamburg on five occasions. From the latter times have come the now legendary Hamburg Tapes which, according to their owner, Allan Williams, would be released during 1977 as a double L.P.

The group underwent various recording auditions and at one, arranged by Decca records, Paul sang the song **Red Sails In The Sunset**. Decca turned the Beatles down, a blunder which went down in music-business folklore as the biggest goof of all time. But the company recovered its shattered dignity a few years later when it snapped up the Rolling Stones. It was EMI who eventually signed the four, save that there was a group change with Ringo Starr (Richard Starkey) replacing Pete Best on drums. The Liverpool music scene into which the Beatles came bore little relation to national trends. The idols of the many Liverpool bands came from America with Chuck Berry and Ray Charles the two most prominently imitated artists. Records by these were not generally found in local stores. They were brought home by merchant seamen who docked at Liverpool.

Group comradeship was strong, but competition fierce. The Beatles played and sang American material but it was the McCartney-Lennon writing partnership which sorted them out from everyone else. Prior to their first recording, the Beatles had some eighty numbers by the duo available for live performance. It was inevitable that they would leave home and seek general British and then world fame. Not all Liverpool fans at the time approved.

As Beatle history shows, the group's first recordings were largely of material other than their own, at least this was true of the album field. In the singles stakes, the Lennon-McCartney partnership flourished. Their first single was **Love Me Do** and **P.S. I Love You**. Paul sang vocal lead on both cuts. In future Beatle terms, the record was only a minor success in Britain, for it reached only seventeen in the Top 20. Two years later, in 1964, the disc was issued in America and topped the charts.

It was the next Beatle single which really began the amazing hit run for Lennon-McCartney. This was **Please Please Me** and for five years the group's sound gave countless other people their direction and ensured a constant hit run for the duo's compositions which only ended with the release of the **Ballad Of John And Yoko** in June of 1969. **Please Please Me** reached number two, the next eleven made number one in Britain. In America, **I Want To Hold Your Hand** was the first Lennon-McCartney chart entry, but with issues on both Vee Jay and Swan, as well as Capitol, there was soon a scramble of the duo's titles in US Top 10. **Please Please Me** and **She Loves You** were amongst the early challengers.

Paul's songwriting ability with John became more noticeable when other artists clamoured to cover their songs and, in particular, looked for album cuts of the four which might make good singles. Two examples in Britain were **Ob-La-Di Ob-La-Da**, a number one hit for Marmalade and a top twenty entry for Bedrocks. With **Michelle**, David and Jonathan had a top twenty hit, with main honours falling to the number one success of The Overlanders. Perhaps, though, countless fans were more conscious of Paul for his good looks, the winning smile, undoubted charm and his particular trademark, the cheeky wink.

In group terms, Paul from early on was very much the PR man. He was the one who excited most fan interest, doubtless because he did the talking, announcing and autograph signing. When Brian Epstein became manager, Paul was suspicious of him at first, but he soon became firm friends with Epstein and the two helped form the professional image of the Beatles.

He wrote both music and words for Beatle songs and Lennon did likewise, but if Paul's songs were often gentle and melodic, he could also belt out a rocker as well as John. Together they formed a powerful stage vocal partnership. Success was there from the moment they set foot on stage. Paul was only 21 on June 18, 1963, and already he and the group, in the space of eight months since the first single release, had toured Britain and Sweden. They had made many television appearances on all the major British shows and in November of 1963 they were billed as part of the traditional Royal Variety Performance, which is held each year in Britain, in the presence of the Royal Family. January of 1964 saw Paul and the other three in America for the first time. They appeared twice on the Ed Sullivan show and performed at concerts in Washington D.C. and New York. They spent a brief holiday in Miami.

Beatlemania in America was under way, and also in Britain, though it was less intense. In America, a vast array of Beatle merchandise could be bought and Paul's face adorned T-shirts, posters, talcum powder tins, wallpaper, stockings, cards and pillows.

The Beatles were soon into films. In 1964, it was **A Hard Day's Night** and a year later, **Help!** 1965 saw the four made individual Members of the Order of the British Empire. British TV featured, under the title of **The Music Of Lennon and McCartney**, a special hour-long TV show and in 1966 Paul composed the sound-track of the British comedy film, **The Family Way**, made

The Beatles at the height of their fame in the mid-1960s. John Lennon, complete with shades, is already beginning to show the unconventional side of his nature. Paul, on the other hand, has fairly short hair compared to the others, although all sport the famous 'mop-top' fringe.

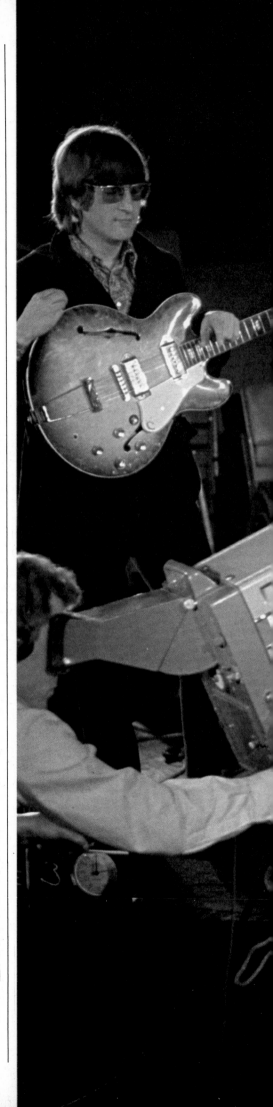

The Beatles' records were always winners and their faces were known worldwide. Their producer was George Martin and they learned from him all about the craft of recording. At this time Paul's permanent girl-friend was actress Jane Asher, who was seen with him everywhere. He also discovered the winsome-voiced Welsh singer, Mary Hopkin. Her single, **Those Were The Days,** was a gigantic number one, but she faded after a few years.

by the Boulting Brothers. The four made their own TV film, **Magical Mystery Tour**. Oddly, the soundtrack was released in America as a lavishly produced album, but its British release only came toward the end of 1976, though countless people bought import copies.

The tensions of Beatle life saw a gradual splitting apart of the Beatles, as each member sought to express his individuality. To one person, John Dunbar, once husband of Marianne Faithful, it was the case of John becoming more and more way-out and Paul restrained by his own caution. Outwardly, Dunbar says, the group appeared united in mid-1960s hipness, but, to him, Paul was increasingly involved in finding his way into the upper-middle class. So it was that, while John Lennon cropped his hair and found his way into Richard Lester's anti-war film, **How I Won The War**, Paul was involved with the Boulting Brothers film. However he did take acid for the first time, though later, after at one time claiming acid led one toward the God-head, he disowned the practice. **Penny Lane** and **Straw-**

berry Fields came out in 1967 and they occupied the charts with their sheer beauty. **Penny Lane** was Paul's composition. Writer Adam Block has called it 'bumptious and whimsical' and for Lennon's **Strawberry Fields** he reserves the words, 'fractured and dizzying'. 1967 was also the time for perhaps rock's most momentous album, **Sgt. Pepper's Lonely Hearts Club Band** and with this album some, as writer Nik Cohn would say that rock 'n' roll lost its soul for many a day.

Outside the immediate music world and its activities Paul, found himself the only Beatle bachelor, though he had formed a close attachment with Jane Asher, and they became engaged. However in August of 1968, at the time of **Hey Jude's** release, the two split. He with the others had become interested in the oriental philosophies of the Maharishi but later they all forsook this particular religious exercise. By the time of the **White Album**, the group had become four distinct individuals. Paul became more and more dominant, partly because he wished to make some sense out of the mess which had arisen from the ill-fated commercial venture, Apple Enterprises. He also had the desire to be on the road again and this passion was partly played out in the film, **Let It Be**, which pictured the Beatles at recording sessions. He also became involved with recording Mary Hopkin, a Welsh girl who had signed with Apple. She found immediate single success, although her album, for which Paul wrote the sleevenotes, did not have a good response. Paul also wrote a song for another Apple signing, Badfinger and took a personal interest in their musical affairs. Their single was **Come And Get It**. It was featured in **The Magic**

Christian, a film which starred Peter Sellers and Ringo. Previous to their first hit, Badfinger were known as The Iveys. One of the group, Joey Molland, their vocalist and guitarist, was thought by some people to be a McCartney look-alike. Some saw McCartney's interest as a kind of father-son relationship, and even if such a thesis seems slightly imaginative, it was enough to interest some musical writers and commentators at the time.

Paul McCartney's increasing leadership within the Beatles set-up did not please everyone, certainly not John. After he saw the final edited version of **Let It Be**, he said, 'I felt sick. That film was set up by Paul *for* Paul.' Lennon said it showed the major reason for the more and more obvious splitting of the Beatles; the other three were fed-up being sidemen for Paul. However, against this it can be said that little would have happened in Beatle territory if Paul had not taken some initiative. In any case, Lennon had been busily pursuing his own interest for some time and this was made particularly clear when Yoko was forever to be seen at Beatle recording sessions. **Let It Be** was released fifteen months after its shooting, and the album only

made its appearance at the time when Paul had already embarked on his solo career. **Abbey Road** had preceeded it.

On March 12, 1969, Paul married Linda Eastman. He suggested that her father and brother should help clear up the Apple mess and take charge of Beatle affairs. The others preferred the American lawyer, Allen Klein. The Beatles breakup soon followed. Nowadays each time a Beatle meets another, as they have done increasingly since

around 1974, the press and general media have assumed a statement of great significance about re-forming must be in the air. To date this has not happened and a possible permanent or temporary Beatle reforming seems as distant as ever. Beatle popularity received a considerable fillip in 1976 with the reactivating of the available Beatle catalogue and on both sides of the Atlantic Beatles singles made chart returns. EMI, UK and Capitol, USA released hitherto album material in

45 form. Both issued **Back In The U.S.S.R.** The Americans released **Got To Get You Into My Life**, a Beatle song recorded and made into a British (1966) hit by Cliff Bennett and The Rebel Rousers and the British issued **Yesterday**, which became a Top 20 hit. Paul, when interviewed at the time, said he was pleased with its success. He spoke warmly of his pleasure at seeing another generation turned on to Beatle music, but said his present sympathies rested with Wings. At that moment in

The Beatles led the trend towards Eastern mysticism, visiting the Indian headquarters of the Maharishi. Paul was the moving spirit behind their television film, **Magical Mystery Tour,** appearing in a bewildering series of disguises.

1976 he had come a long way from the 14 year-old who taught John Lennon some chords on his guitar. There is endless mileage yet in the story of James Paul McCartney.

Linda McCartney

Linda McCartney was formerly Linda Eastman. She comes from a successful and powerful New York family who, among other things, have been involved with the music business. She is herself a talented photographer and has had several volumes of her photographic work published. At one time she was the staff photographer at New York's legendary rock hall, Fillmore East. She met Paul during a London photographic assignment in the late 1960s and the two were married on March 12, 1969. She had one child from a previous marriage.

The marriage was ill-received by many Paul McCartney fans and some music writers were none too polite. Adam Block wrote, 'Linda Eastman, the daughter of a successful New York lawyer/banker, had forsaken the Scarsdale debutante set to become a rock photographer/groupie. Paul once called her "an instant dessert, a royal cream pudding".'

Linda's marriage has, by all accounts, been a great success. She is with Paul constantly, whether on stage, in a recording studio or merely passing the time of day. She has been described as a very loving, close, warm person. One of Linda's habits during the first touring days of Wings was to leave the stage and take photographs of Paul from the front. Also in those early days she was observed as someone who heartily applauded McCartney's performance on certain songs, one in particular being **Maybe I'm Amazed**.

Paul wrote for their engagement the song **Two Of Us**, which he and John Lennon sang in the film, **Let It Be.** Other particular songs written for Linda by Paul have been **My Love; Oh, I Love The Lovely Linda** and **Cook Of The House**, the first solo she has sung on record.

Several early post-Beatle songs by Paul are also credited with Linda's name. The best known is the hit, **Another Day**. Linda has written a number of songs, but, with few exceptions, she describes them in hesitant tones. There have been frequent rumours of a Linda single, partly because the lady herself first spoke of such a project in 1971. After her Jamaican visit with Paul she wrote **Seaside Woman** and, if the record had appeared, it would have been under the make-believe name of 'Suzi and the Red Stripes'. Linda found herself called Suzi during the Jamaica sojourn and Red Stripe is the name for that country's beer.

The B-side of **Seaside Woman** would have had the musical colouring of Linda's love for 1950s R & B, typified by groups like the Penguins and the Doves. The song remains in Linda's self-penned collection without title.

Linda's close musical involvement with Paul, from the moment they met, has left people both speechless in amazement and vocal in criticism. She worked with Paul on his albums **McCartney** and **Ram**, particularly on back-up vocals. However, Linda has no previous musical experience and, although she is now a competent member of Wings, in the early days she had no idea how to play any instrument. As late as 1975, the *Village Voice* writer, Blair Sabol, wrote of his being asked by Linda to come and watch her play during re-mixing of the **Venus and Mars** album in the Wally Heider studio, Los Angeles. He found her ability virtually nil. Sabol said, 'She sat down, struck two notes, jumped up and was on to the moog. She hit four moog groans and went on to a guitar. She didn't complete one riff on one instrument nor did she complete one explanatory statement.' Linda's progress has been due to Paul's unswerving belief in her and in his own musical policy for Wings. He also made the definite decision of not defending his action in media circles. He told Hunter Davis in the colour supplement of Britain's *Sunday Times*, 'I don't have to explain her away. She's my wife and I want her to play . . . I decided not to defend Linda; let them find out what we were trying to do. I said nothing, just as I said nothing during all John's tirades against me.'

During early Wings' concerts, Linda visibly shook with nerves and at times her hands visibly froze with fear. It seemed quite a different Linda during the 1975–6 World Tour, for she imparted a star image and a sense of ease with the vast array of instruments for which she is musically responsible. Wings member Denny Laine has said Linda possesses a good ear for music and that she takes full part in group ideas. He agreed with the validity of the initial criticism of Linda's musicianship, but believes strongly, as does Paul, that people did not fully understand where the band was heading.

A few weeks before Christmas, 1975 the book *Linda's Pix for Seventy-Six* was published in Britain by Jonathan Cape. This contains not only pictures of Paul and family, Wings and personnel but also shots of such notables as Jimi Hendrix, Bob Dylan and John Lennon. British reviews were kind and generous in their praise.

Denny Laine

Denny Laine has been with Paul since the group's inception. He was an original Moody Blues member, way back in 1964 when the band was basically into R & B music. With the group he recorded the song **Go Now** which was a British number one, early in 1965. In April of the same year, the record reached number ten in the American *Billboard* chart. Subsequent Moody Blues records made less impact and Laine, along with Clint Warwick, left the group.

Laine's, Moody Blues era has become

Linda came into Paul's life around the time of the Beatles breakup. He encouraged her to become a singer and musician.

part of Wings lore, with his regular performance of **Go Now**. His singing of this song is found on the triple-record album, **Wings Over America**. Another famous Laine song composition is **Say You Don't Mind**, perhaps the most positive thing which came from the short time Laine spent fronting the Electric String Band. The song was recorded in 1967 but meant nothing in British chart terms until Colin Blunstone's epic recording of the song reached number fifteen in the March charts of 1972. In 1969, Laine was part of Balls, a group he formed with ex-Move member, Trevor Burton. The group managed ten gigs and recorded one disc for the British market entitled, **Fight For My Country**. At the same time as Balls, Laine guested with Ginger Baker's Airforce. In 1971 he joined up with Paul and so extended into tangible form his respect and affection for McCartney's musical ideas. Laine once said, 'I think I've got some idea of the way he feels about things and I know the kind of pressure he's under because I've been through a lot of the same stuff myself. The longer you go on the tougher it is in lots of ways. People expect more and more of you. For Paul, having been part of the best rock 'n' roll band in history, it must be very heavy. I admire him so much.'

Paul, for his part, has often spoken in similarly warm terms of Denny. In one instance, at the time of press interviews for the release date of **Wings – Wild Life**, Paul expressed his admiration for Denny's voice, a feeling which went back to his hearing Denny's vocal on **Go Now**. He also spoke highly of Denny's guitar playing.

Laine has always insisted Wings is Wings and not McCartney revisited. He once said, 'You know, Paul with his reputation could have come back and played all the old Beatle numbers associated with him. It would have been easy.' Laine, like the others, was very

conscious of initial criticism. He said, 'We had our teething troubles as a group and, sure, there were many critics coming along and writing searing stuff in the pop press. I don't mind what they do. I thrive on criticism and it gives me the urge to prove them wrong.'

Denny confesses his deep love for music. He once said, 'I'll be 97 when I play my last number, but then I don't think I'll ever die'. On another occasion he said, 'Music is me: gigging is me', and he compared Moody Blues days with those of Wings, in the words, 'I just dig those songs Wings play. I was very much into the early Moody stuff. Later it became all very serious and bored me a bit. I want more immediate music, something you can really get involved with. Paul has this running right through him.' He just smiles when he hears of groups who aim to reach the state where they think they can sit back, finish the live stuff and merely release one or two albums a year. He is constantly concerned with improving his musical standards and when he works with anyone, then he expects them to have a high musical standard. He describes himself as a non-pushing kind of individual and he has seen himself gradually moving into a more central position within the Wings set-up. His solo album, titled, **Ahh . . . Laine!** took several years in the making. The production was by Tony Secunda and it was basically an album expressing his desire to 'do the singer-songwriter bit. I play about everything on the album.' Whilst the album received some pleasant reviews, the disc made little impact on the general public and it soon became lost amid the usual monthly mass of LP releases.

During 1976 Paul McCartney acquired for his company the publishing rights of all Buddy Holly's songs and in Britain a special Buddy Holly week was held. Laine recorded a single of the song **It's So Easy**, but it made no chart impact. In 1977, the album, **Hollydays**, was issued. It comprised Denny singing and playing songs associated with Buddy Holly.

Laine, in spite of his musical passion, does have other interests. He has a fascination with cars. One of his prized possessions is a Jaguar 3.8 which, according to him, had no need of service until it had clocked 50,000 miles.

Denny Laine, ex-member of the Moody Blues, is a very old friend of Paul. Like him, he loves playing on stage and is devoted to a peaceful family life. He has been with Wings from the beginning.

Jimmy McCulloch

Jimmy McCulloch has become an increasingly impressive figure within the Wings line-up. His major record contributions for Wings are **Medicine Jar** from the **Venus and Mars** album and, on **Wings At The Speed of Sound, Wino Junko**.

Jimmy began his career as a working musician at the age of 13. He came into musical prominence as part of the Thunderclap Newman band which had a British number one hit in 1969 with **Something In The Air**. The disc reached number 37 in the United States. On leaving Thunderclap Newman, McCulloch played with John Mayall and then with Stone The Crows. He joined the latter band in 1972 as replacement for Les Harvey. The band broke up in 1973. Some of McCulloch's work with the band is on a British-released compilation album of the group's recordings from 1970 to 1972. The album, **Transparency Processed**, was issued by UK Polydor in 1976.

McCulloch joined Wings at the time of their Nashville recording sessions in 1974. In an interview at the end of November, 1976, McCulloch said, 'Wings are settled for years, it would be a shame if anything happened. I can't see anything cracking Wings in the foreseeable future.' At the completion of Wings' World Tour in 1976, McCulloch indulged in a spate of press and radio interviews which revealed his association with an occasional band of friends called White Line. McCulloch described the affair as 'fun'. A single was issued by British EMI entitled, **Call My Name**. McCulloch thought an album and further singles were likely but he stressed that White Line only existed as a refreshing musical exercise while Wings was off the road.

Joe English

Joe is an American from Rochester, New York. He was recommended to Paul by American arranger and trombonist, Tony Dorsey. He drummed for Wings during **Venus and Mars** recording sessions in 1975. Previous to this, he had gained a reputation as a fine session musician at Georgia's Atlanta stuios. He had toured with Hendrix, Janis Joplin and The Grateful Dead and immediately before joining the Wings' recordings, was working with Bonnie Bramlett. English impressed Paul McCartney with his drumming and, when invited to join the band, he readily accepted. It turned out that he, in common with both Denny and Jimmy, had always been a Beatle fan and this musical love had made him familiar with some of McCartney's musical traits. English replaced a British drummer, Geoff Britton in the group line-up. The correctness of McCartney's choice was shown clearly during the many

gigs Wings played during 1975 and 1976 and on many occasions his solid, powerful drumming was praised by musical critics.

Other Band Members:
The initial band line-up in 1971 for **Wild Life** was Paul, Linda, Denny and Denny Seiwell. Seiwell was a respected New York session musician. He auditioned for Wings when **Ram** was being recorded in New York. Each prospective band member was asked to perform a simple rock 'n' roll beat. Paul said most drummers would reach for the high-hat when he led them in. Denny, unlike the others, went straight for the tom-toms and, within seconds, the room throbbed with his sound. Paul said he was sold on Seiwell's ability and he found him technically a good drummer with a useful bass voice. Seiwell left the Band after the British tour of 1973. He and his French wife, Monique, bought themselves a farm in Scotland and like Paul, also owned a house in London. During an interview in April, 1973, he went out of his way to say Wings was an 'English' band and he professed an enjoyment of English life: even English football. Seiwell described Wings – '73, as a band of rockers with the object of having and giving a good time.

Guitarist, Henry McCullough left at the same time as Seiwell. McCullough had joined the band at the time of **Red Rose Speedway**, 1973. He had formerly been with the Grease Band.

Another brief band member was Geoff Britton. Britton, like Jimmy McCulloch, joined at the time of the Nashville, U.S.A. recordings, from which came the hit single, **Junior's Farm**. Britton, a karate expert, was enthusiastic about joining Wings. The romance did not last long and he was eventually replaced by Joe English.

Apart from the band members, there is a vast entourage of people involved with administration and the general running of the band's musical affairs. The kingpin figure is Brian Brolly, who is Managing Director of Paul's own company, McCartney Productions.

Brolly declares that the purpose of the organization is not simply to manage Paul's affairs, but to do so 'honestly, morally and with integrity'. One of the more colourful people involved with Wings is the group's long-standing publicist, Tony Brainsby. Brainsby ensures constant Wings' coverage in the print and visual media.

At the commencement of 1977 Wings comprised Paul and Linda McCartney, Denny Laine, Joe English and Jimmy McCulloch. This was the same line-up as that of early, 1975.

Jimmy McCulloch was a child prodigy of rock who was a professional musician at the age of fifteen. Drummer Joe English, an American from Rochester, New York, joined Wings after **Venus and Mars** and soon settled down as a member of the group.

4
THE WORLD TOUR
1975-1976

London's Empire Pool, Wembley, seats 8,000. Wings booked three dates in 1976 from October 19 to 21. Tickets were sold within three days. The same story could well be told worldwide. McCartney magic worked, but by the end of each concert people were also conscious of Wings as a group.

The triumphant world tour lasted, with some interruptions, for thirteen months. The planning was an enormous task, with so many things which could go wrong, from hotel bookings to pieces of the 12½ tons of equipment going astray. And even if those aspects of the tour operated faultlessly there was still the tricky business of ensuring there was a good sound in whatever hall or stadium was the chosen venue. Every rock band on tour encounters problems, which is why they all have crews of expert 'roadies', skilled in overcoming technical crises without fuss. In the case of Wings, the first crisis came on the very first show of their World Tour. Southampton's Gaumont cinema (movie-house) did not have a specially prepared space for the enormous P.A. control-board which they use. The crew built a temporary structure which rested somewhat precariously on rear stalls seats. Other problems which a band crew can find sometimes have their source in one very basic difficulty. They may not even be able to get some of their stuff into the building without taking it to pieces, and this can be very time-consuming and tiring, particularly when the band gigs at a different location each day.

In spite of such problems, the Wings road crew worked faultlessly and with considerable skill. Their abilities complimented those of the band. The band arrived to carry out their sound-check, usually around 5 p.m. in full confidence things would be ready for them. They also knew that security matters received proper attention and that people could see properly, though at London's Wembley concert there were some problems, for the stage speakers prevented some people from really seeing the stage-front, even though many seats to both sides of the arena's stage had not been sold for this very reason. Here, Paul and the band went out of their way to stand at positions where people could see as much of the action as possible, and both Paul and Linda frequently went across and made a special fuss of those who might not have had the best-placed seats. Of course, even during the actual concert, many things can go wrong. Here a band relies heavily on good roadies who can attend within seconds to a fault which may have developed in the amplification system or a particular musical instrument.

Since Wings travelled enormous distances during their World Tour, there were heavy shipment costs involved. The cost of shipping the show's equipment from Dallas to London for example, was enormous. The total weight came to 9072kg, at a freight cost of

$1.50 per kg, which means $13,608. There are additional handling charges, the trucking from location source to the airport and vice-versa, equipment insurance, crew members and their air tickets which, in the end, leaves little from £10,000. Britain's Hammersmith Odeon, a venue of around 4,000 seating capacity, filled for two nights, would not even pay for the transportation.

For all concert dates, Wings had an extra horn section. The personnel was Tony Dorsey, trombone, Thaddeus Richard, soprano and alto saxophones, clarinet, flute and piccolo, Howie Casey, tenor saxophone and Steve 'Tex' Howard, trumpet and flugelhorn. They were superb. Casey hails from Liverpool and has been Paul's friend from teen days. Dorsey was responsible for the horn section arrangements and led the band. His background includes work with Joe Tex and he helped Paul with some sections of **Venus and Mars**. It was he who suggested session musicians Thaddeus and Steve for the final horn section line-up.

The first part of the world tour took in most major cities in Britain. What was established in this initial 13-gig British itinerary laid the foundations for all other concerts. The structure of the musical side was based on songs from the various albums with some emphasis upon the most popular items. As the album **Wings Across America** shows, the mood was set at the outset with the haunting opening of the **Venus and Mars** L.P. Paul would sing some Beatle numbers and at one point in the show the band would come and sit on chairs placed in a semi-circle at the front of the stage, to play and sing their way through an 'acoustic' set. Denny Laine and Jimmy McCulloch would also have their own solo spots. The only person not specifically featured was Joe English, but English proved himself to be an indispensible member of the band with his faultless drumming.

Venus and Mars cuts were usually followed by the excellent, exciting **Jet** and the next, **Call Me Back Again.** Other numbers featured were **Silly Love Songs, Hi Hi Hi, Let 'Em In, My Love** and **Live and Let Die.** Denny, of course, sang **Go Now** and Jimmy played some pulsating guitar riffs, on **Time To Hide**, which also featured Denny on lead vocals.

Paul delighted audiences wherever the band played, and his Beatle set was warmly received not only by the Beatle generation, but by fans much too young to remember the Fab Four. He sang numbers like **Yesterday, Lady Madonna** and **The Long Winding Road.** And, in the case of the last two, he sang them even better than the original version.

The McCartney family always stick together, even on tour. They travelled America in a specially chartered jet. There are always games to help them relax between shows and plenty of fooling around.

Wings kept a basic format throughout their world tour but, from time to time, the song selection was changed. Each show lasted around two to two-and-a-half hours. Each concert began just about on time, not a common occurance in the rock-pop world. At London's Wembley, numerous fans streamed in late. Doubtless they assumed from their normal concert-going experience that the event would not start on time and that they would be given an unasked-for 'support' group.

A piece of criticism, which may be justified, lies in the band's lack of musical surprise. Sometimes they knew their lines a little too well and they did not make each other work hard enough. Yet, for all that, it was a vintage Wings who could reproduce so brilliantly and continuously, night after night, complex numbers like **Live and Let Die**, as if one were indeed sitting there in the Abbey Road studios hearing the final mix.

Wings are undoubtedly professional in the true, some would say old-fashioned, sense of the word. Their professionalism, for example, showed in the sound balance at their concerts, which was sometimes quite unbelievable in its clarity and mix. There were even moments which sounded better than the studio-recorded version.

This amazing sound-reproduction was the work of Jack Maxson, Morris Lyda and Craig Schertz who came with the 'Showco' equipment system, whose factory is in Dallas, Texas. The whole operation was under the direction of Paul McCartney's technical right-hand man, Trevor Jones. Linda alone has quite a battery of instruments, all of which must be carefully programmed and made ready. They consist of a Fender-Rhodes Electric Piano, A Mellotron, a C3 Hammond Organ, an ARP Synthesizer, a Hohner Clavinet and a Mini-Moog Synthesizer. The most sensitive of these is The Mellotron, which, if it goes wrong, can mean a complicated sorting out of a jammed tape.

Some 37 guitars, it seems, could be called into use during a concert and on top of this there is Joe's gear. It was amazing that things went without a hitch and at the end of each day there were happy musicians and satisfied audiences. On the American section of the world tour Wings travelled in a chartered BAC one-eleven. Inside, the plane was fitted out like a living room, with the plane's outside bearing the tour motto, 'Wings Over America'. On board they took with them various items to pass the time. A table-tennis table, table-football and a dartboard were three items which proved welcome relaxations and these pastimes were hauled around the various halls and theatres. America gave Wings a mar-

The cameras are always pointed, both on stage and off. Literally miles of film are shot by press photographers during a tour, although only a few are ever published.

vellous reception and in the Kingdome, Seattle, the band played before 67,000 people, establishing the largest indoor concert attendance of all time. A huge colour-video screen which was hung above the band enabled the large crowd to have an excellent view. Few of them could have realized that the stage on which they saw Wings had in fact taken three days to build.

The Seattle show began with a slight disaster when a fireworks flare which was fired the whole length of the stadium decided to jam near the stage but by the end this was forgotten as thousands of fans lapped up the music. Seattle came as the U.S. tour's 19th destination. For Paul, it was a nostalgic event. The memories of touring America with the Beatles in 1966 must have been strong in his mind. And there were, of course those who constantly recalled the event by making predictions of Beatles 1977 or flashing more and more grotesque sums of money the way of Paul and the other Beatles. Paul continually parried questions on a Beatles comeback, sometimes getting noticeably impatient with them.

Paul had started the American part of the World Tour with a little trepidation, as had Linda. Linda worried over whether the socially oriented American music-journal *Rolling Stone* would find her wanting, musically. As she said to Hunter Davies of Britain's *Sunday Times* before the first American tour, 'I'd love to put the critics up there on stage and see them do better. You lose a few years of your life on stage. You live on your adrenalin. When it's over I want to crash out and go and live in

Scotland for a while. We've got to do America to prove we can do it.'

The powerful U.S. music trade magazine *Billboard*, must have given her some heart, for they commented that she served a key role in the band. As for Paul, *Billboard* thought his voice had become sweeter and more powerful, and showed no signs of faltering. *Billboard*'s writer, Jim Fishel, reported

that Wings featuring Paul McCartney had blasted into New York on May 24 and had given the standing-room-only crowd at Madison Square Garden a taste of what Beatlemania had been like in its heyday. Fishel saw McCartney's own future 'blooming'. In particular, he praised the drumming of Joe English and commented that English showed quite plainly that there is no need for

two bass drums and three tom-toms in order to be effective. He said English was always on cue and kept the band together, never getting in the way of McCartney's melodies.

The crowd was frequently raised to fever pitch and, for Fishel, some of the best times were found in the updated version of **I've Just Seen A Face**, a stirring **Lady Madonna** from Paul,

Denny's lead vocals on **Spirits of Ancient Egypt** and **Richard Cory**, the 1930s feel on **You Gave Me The Answer**, the tasty horn riffs on **Let 'Em In** and Joe's drumming on **My Love**. This was a very together band.

Wherever they went, Wings gathered rave notices from the press. Gary Mc-Donald, of the *Dallas Iconoclast*, felt there was even the best yet to come

A regular feature of the Wings show is the 'acoustic set', when the band sit at the front of the stage. It is during this part of the show that Paul sings **Yesterday.**

from Wings. People would have to work, he wrote, if they were going to find reason for complaint after this concert. He found the show well paced

For the press the entire trip was dominated by a rumour which they themselves had created: "Will there be a Beatles reunion?" The mere fact that all the Fab Four were on the same continent at the same time was enough to set speculation flying. Ticket touts were reportedly asking £200 for £8 tickets on the strength of the proposed on-stage meeting and every concert report added fuel to the fire. It was a classic example of manufactured news. No-one had actually said that any such event was likely to take place. Nothing irks McCartney more than questions about a reunion, and he finally knocked it all on the head with a Mohammed Ali-type verse:

The Beatles split in '69
And since then they have been doing fine
And if that question doesn't cease
Ain't no-one gonna get no peace
And if they ask it just once more
I think I'll have to bash their jaw.

The nearest it ever came was on 23rd June in Los Angeles, when Ringo got up on stage, gave Paul a bouquet of flowers, picked up a guitar and waved it around his head... applause so much for press speculation.

Naturally, there were celebrities, rock stars like Elton John, Rod Stewart, Linda Ronstadt and Brian Wilson, actors like Tony Curtis and Jack Nicholson... like Jackie Onassis famous for being famous and their pictures taken, but it was only a sideshow. The real stuff was taking place on stage as Wings went through their immaculate performances before thousands of fans, at least half of whom were too young to remember the Beatles and loved the band simply for what they were.

Wings and Ringo
on stage in Los Angeles

and musically tight, and the lights and other effects were very impressive. He singled out McCulloch's guitar licks on **Maybe I'm Amazed** and found the band's version of **Live And Let Die** to have even more impact than the recorded version. He was particularly impressed with numbers from **Band On The Run**, but had some reservations about material from **Venus and Mars**. In the case of the former, he found the songs gained even greater impact in live performance.

The *Long Island Press* reporter, William Barber went overboard with praise for the Wings concert at Nassau Coliseum. He began his copy with the words, 'We weren't sure before, but now we're convinced – Paul McCartney isn't human after all. Any man who can do what Paul does with his music has got to be an exalted wizard.' Barber was fascinated by the 'eye-popping visual effects created by lighting designs, film-slides and whatever else'. He called it all 'mind-boggling'. For him, the concert was the year's best event.

At Los Angeles there was almost hysteria when Ringo suddenly got up on stage and presented Paul with a bouquet of flowers. However he was not followed by George and John, even though the two were in America. If one is impressed by celebrity listings as a sign of a group or artist's standing, then Wings shows attracted people like Brian Wilson of The Beach Boys, actor Jack Nicholson and the rich and famous, like Jackie Onassis.

The American tour ended on June 23, after three gigs in Los Angeles. The next booking was on September 19 at the Stadthalle, Vienna and from there, the band journeyed onwards to the Dom Sportova Hall, Zagreb, Yugoslavia. Here Paul was amazed at the reception given the band, for he expected things to be rather dour. Instead, he found crowds quite 'loony', to quote his own word.

The much publicized UNESCO event in St. Mark's Square, Venice was on September 25, 1976. The temperature was 90 degrees. Venice has long been dying from decay and neglect and, around the mid-late 1960s, the city politicians decided a special financial appeal was needed to save the historic city. Many buildings had been badly affected in recent times by flood waters. In September '76, a series of concerts was held with the purpose of making people aware of the city's troubles. Mort Shumann, Peter Ustinov, Ravi

Touring is an exhausting business. There are fans, press and photographers wherever Wings go and they are always on show whatever the time of day or night and regardless of the way they feel at the time. The families usually manage to get together in the dressing room before the show. While their parents are being rock stars on the stage the children are in bed, fast asleep. It is an ordinary, regular life for them.

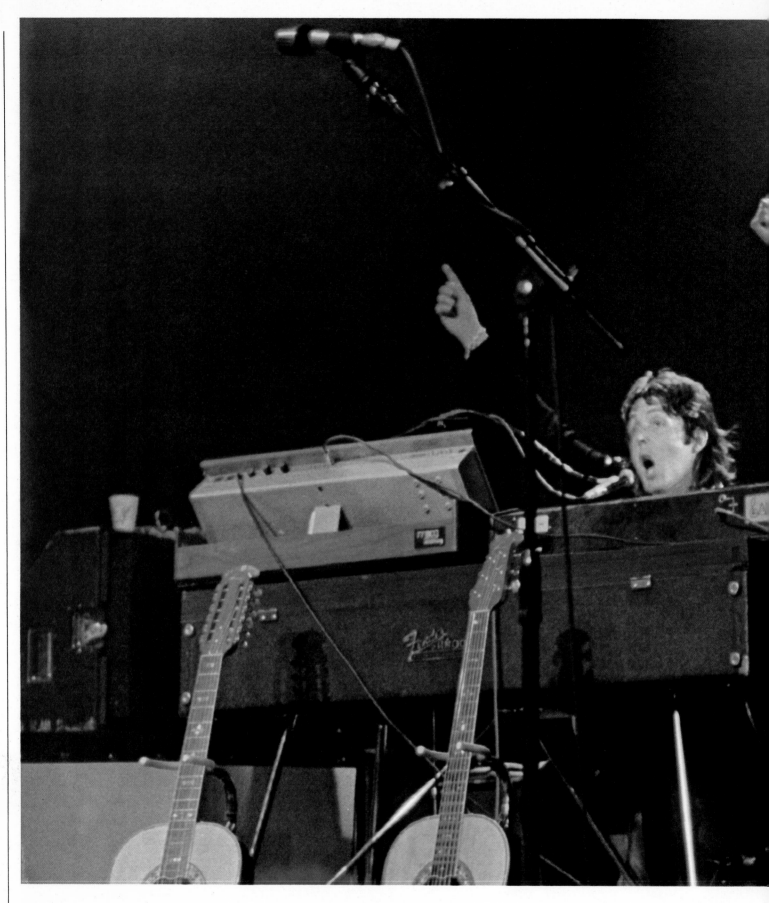

Shankar and the La Chunga Flamenco Ballet were some of those who gave their services. With young people in mind, the city authorities approached Wings, the band agreed to finance the concerts themselves. Strict limits were imposed on crowd-size and equipment weight, since the Piazza stands on wooden piles which are sunk into the sea bed.

The Press had been given special seats and the authorities had strictly controlled the number of seats in front of the stage. Their reason for doing so lay in their fear that too much weight in the immediate stage area might cause a disaster. As it happened, some people saw it as a ruse to separate the poor from the favoured rich. They took matters into their own hands and by sheer weight of numbers and aggression took control of the especially allotted seats. 30,000 people, of all ages and types, turned up for the historic rock concert and heard Wings play virtually the same set as they had been playing during their World Tour.

At first the band were slow getting into their stride, even though **Jet** came early, but tempo was slackened by the inclusion of **Let Me Roll It**. There were solos from Jimmy and Denny and then Paul at the grand piano sang and

played his great song, **Maybe I'm Amazed**. The concert stepped into top gear with McCartney's energetic performance of **Lady Madonna**, and a well-received version of **The Long And Winding Road**, with the horn section more than compensating for the heavy string version which can be found on the album, **Let It Be. Yesterday** was received with Beatle-days ecstasy. McCartney smiled a great deal

and Denny Laine looked happy, though somewhat frustrated that the crowd didn't clap as vigorously as he desired. There were two encores, **Hi Hi Hi** and **Soily**. For the visual finale, the laser shone its way towards the red brick clock tower at the opposite end of the Piazza from the stage, before it eventually formed itself into the 'W' for Wings emblem. The UNESCO event was over. A success and a credit to the

Paul and Linda put every ounce of energy into their show. It is a non-stop production and everything must be perfect.

band, it was one of their finest occasions.

The World Tour had begun in Britain and there it ended with the amazingly successful Wembley concerts. Everything went right, and it was the perfect homecoming for a band which must

71

now rank as one of the best in the world.

Wembley had the air of something big about to happen. People swapped versions of wild rumours which suggested that the Beatle four would be reunited on this stage, even if they only hugged or shook hands. There were people of McCartney's generation with their young children, for whom the Beatles were names on Daddy's record sleeves. There were teenagers who were fans of Wings, and people who just looked curious or realized the Wembley Wings concerts were the most sought-after events in London. The show began just after eight, in this somewhat cold and barren stadium, which houses just about everything during the year, from trade exhibitions to ice hockey. McCartney and Wings obviously loved being home and received rapturous applause from beginning to end. McCartney joked and egged the crowd on. He had them singing bird noises on **Blackbird** and asked, on the first evening, whether there were any Americans in the audience. There were some but not too many. He then asked whether there were British people present. There was immediate uproar. The Liverpool lad was home in England. Maybe he would

The family walked around St Mark's Square, Venice, before their charity concert there for UNESCO. The Italian crowd went wild with delight that evening as Wings gave one of the greatest performances of their career. By this time, with months of touring behind them, they were full of confidence and clowned around happily. The end of the long journey was in sight.

have preferred Liverpool and Merseyside, but Wembley loved him.

The band looked relaxed and even Linda appeared radiant and confident, as if all her worries about being in the band, being on tour and visiting America had now vanished. There were even some people chanting her name and, as Sheila Prophet wondered in her review for *Record Mirror*, 'Can she actually be gaining her own fan following?'

Linda and Paul frequently waved at the crowd in appreciation and it was one of those concerts when helpers, ushers, stewards, camera crews and photographers stayed inside the hall in large bunches long after the show was over. The only discordant note was raised by the Greater London Council's strict safety and security arrangements

which meant some house lights being kept on. This rather spoilt the dramatic lighting tricks, which needed total darkness if they were to have their full effect.

By the end of the three Wembley nights, Wings had toured ten countries and played 62 concerts in ten months. The tour had achieved the re-establishment of Paul McCartney as a world pop figure and Wings had joined the small list of top flight live bands. Wings slept soundly after their third and final Wembley concert was over. They had achieved everything they had set out to do and few bands have ever done that.

At the end of the show Paul and Linda acknowledge the cheers of the crowd. They always had to come back on stage for an encore before the audience would go home. The album **Wings Over America** is evidence of the tremendous response they had wherever they appeared on the world tour.

5
PAUL AND LINDA — THE FAMILY WAY

Wings were on tour. One afternoon someone noticed the McCartneys were missing. Eventually, late in the afternoon, they drifted into the hotel where everyone was staying. The bottom of Paul's trousers seemed wet and his shoes were covered with sand. He and Linda had gone off to the seaside and taken with them their three children, Heather, Mary and Stella. And what other famous group is there which has a mum and dad in its line-up who take their kids with them wherever they go? And decides the afternoon would be best spent mixing with the general public on a beach?

When the band played Denmark, in 1975, Paul and family decided they would go and see the Danish Queen. So they arrived at the palace and said, 'Hello, we're the McCartneys and we've come to see the Queen.' As it happened the Queen was out, but the visit ensured one thing; they were loved by the Danish press who appreciated the friendliness and respect. For some people, of course, it's strange that there should be a world-rated group which has this cosy family atmosphere. The Americans probably find it much easier to comprehend than the British. After all, the Americans have had many family groups and for them the two things, having a family and being in the music business, can co-exist without one or the other suffering as a consequence. Some British people, though, are puzzled. If they were not, then one of the country's highest circulation Sunday papers would not have thought

Although Linda was criticized during the early days, Paul has always had faith in her ability as a musician. 'I don't need to make excuses for her,' he says firmly. Paul and Linda are always together. Whatever they do – travelling, relaxing or making music – they do as a team. Their family are always with them. Probably as many pictures are published of the McCartneys as a family as of them as rock stars.

it newsworthy to have on its front-page the happy family which has pop stars as parents. They found the story of a happily married man who has a splendid, loving wife and three kids, who reflect in their own happiness the joy felt by their parents. Usually, the newspapers reveal less happy private lives in the world of pop. Linda has said time and again that she and Paul exist for two things, apart from their personal love – their music and their children. Wherever they go, they take

the children with them. Heather is the eldest and, when Wings were preparing for the US tour in 1976, Paul asked her whether she would rather stay at home. After all, she had already travelled half-way around the world with the band. But Heather wouldn't hear of it. She chose the tour.

When they are on tour, the McCartney's ensure that life is as comfortable as possible. They hired three houses in America, one on each coast and another in the mid-west. This arrangement made

it possible to go 'home' every night instead of staying in hotels. You can, of course, only commute like this if you've got a jet handy.

The McCartneys run two homes, one in London, the other in Scotland. They visit their families in Liverpool and New York, and usually have an American Christmas and a British New Year. One American Christmas they took the kids to The Wilderness Family and attended a George Harrison concert. They simply do what any

other well-off family might do in the American city. If they are staying in Los Angeles, they meet and visit the many pop stars who live there.

Linda enjoys the Scottish residence. She values the times they have together on their farm and loves to talk about such homely matters as fruit-bottling or the recent crops of potatoes and carrots. One British journalist, David Robson, editor of a magazine called *Honey*, expressed his amazement that, even within sight of a concert stage,

you can find Paul and Linda chatting away to people about the state of their children's teeth. Within twenty seconds the two are on stage and Wings have launched into **Venus and Mars**. Paul's wife adores farmyard animals and some of these even populate their more sedate London residence. The house is located in St. John's Wood, a rather wealthy area, not far from both Abbey Road, the home of the EMI recording studios, and London's West End shopping streets. Their house is an attractive

Martha, his old English sheep dog, is one of Paul's best friends. He wrote **Martha My Dear** about her.

Regency mansion with a definite air of homeliness everywhere. Children's toys and games lie all over the place with a delightful casualness. Linda also believes that, wherever they are, one thing is important, namely that Paul should have a good breakfast. The menu more often than not is fried eggs,

Paul was born into a close and loving family, and it is the model for his way of life today. Some people think that it is a strange way for a rock star to act, but he is absolutely genuine about it. If he had not been the idol of millions he would have been the same. His fans admire him for sticking to what he wants in life and the McCartneys live as they please. They couldn't do otherwise. Homelife with the children and animals matters to Linda and Paul.

bacon and fried bread. Linda's love for a fry-up has been immortalized for all time with the track, **Cook Of The House** on the **Wings At The Speed Of Sound** album.

The McCartney household contains a lady-help, Rose, who takes care of the children when professional duties must occupy the attention of Paul and Linda. However, even if Rose is with them on tour, Linda will still ensure she does the cooking herself on many evenings. The McCartneys believe it is important that the three girls should see plenty of their parents.

There are also particular favourite animals which are regarded as true McCartneys. There are four dogs and one is Martha, an eleven year old English sheepdog who appears on the song, **Martha My Dear**. And there is **Jet**. The McCartneys have a Labrador bitch who one day came back from

her travels pregnant and gave birth to seven puppies. One of the puppies was named Jet. They even have a name for their Land Rover – 'Helen Wheels' a typical McCartney pun, referring to the slogan which was often painted on the sides of World War II vehicles, 'Hell On Wheels'. It takes them everywhere and the story of its travels is told in the song of the same name, where the journey takes the family just about the length and breadth of the British Isles, outside of the far South-West. Paul, apart from riding a moped around the farm, playing with the children and performing necessary routine duties demanded from someone who owns land, enjoys science fiction and comic books. He will very occasionally venture forth into the concert and party world. McCartney is an easy person to talk with. He is affable and has no affectations. If Linda is with him, she usually has her arm around his waist and she listens intently to what he is saying.

It has been obvious from this chapter that Paul loves children. Of his own, Linda says, 'He really enjoys children. He doesn't have to work at it . . .' But his love goes further than his own kids, for many stories have filtered through of his kindness to kids he can't even know, yet because they are young he instinctively likes and can communicate with them. It's been said that even

if Paul plays before 8,000 people in a large hall, he will get more satisfaction over pleasing a handful of young kids in the audience than delighting the thousands of adults. And if they are near the front of the stage and he spots them, then he will go out of his way to make them particularly welcome with his famous smile and wink. People have wandered into recording sessions and found the maestro busily eating lunch with a bunch of studio personnel's children. Not that being considerate and kind to children, affable and friendly as a person, means Paul is a push-over. He is certainly not lax when it comes to standards. Many a person has commented on Paul's musical commitment and this is nothing less than a relentless search for perfection; he expects those who work with him to have the highest standards. In this he can sometimes be intolerant. Henry McCullough has commented that sometimes he or the others would be afraid to say they have this or that song, simply because of 'McCartneyism'.

As a father, Paul comes across with magnetism, very much in the traditional role of the man who believes it's his duty to care for his wife and children. And he would see it as his right to make decisions and know where things are heading.

Linda, in public, gives the impression

of not only being devoted to Paul and the children but of assuming a secondary position. Yet this can be deceptive for, in a muscial sense, even if she is not as talented as Paul, she has always from the start been a consultant and mutual music-maker. And she does make decisions; the proposal for recording in Lagos came from her and, on a purely domestic level, it is she who rigidly preserves her role as mother, when paid help is readily available.

While preserving their family stability within the context of Wings and touring, and seeing it flourish in the context of their two British homes, both Paul and Linda still find time for their own special projects. Linda has her love for photography, though most is of Wings and their own family, and Paul frequently pops up with recording or film projects. He worked on his own brother's solo album and with Scaffold. When Geoff Britton was Wing's drummer, he represented Britain against Japan at karate. Paul filmed the whole event and wrote the soundtrack for professional showing. He has also been closely involved with the Denny Laine–Buddy Holly saga, in single and album form. And though in the early part of the 1970s things with Ringo were not too amicable, since the two have resumed their friendship, Paul has worked with Ringo on disc. McCartney plays kazoo on Ringo's, **You're Sixteen**, his version of the old Johnny Burnette hit. And on the album **Ringo**, Paul contributed the song, **Six O'Clock** and another track was penned by Lennon, Ringo, George. It's been the nearest to a Beatle get-together and some at the time said, Paul or no Paul, it could have been the new Beatles.

McCartney says he has few really close friends. One real mate is, of course, Denny Laine. Time and time again, during general press interviews, Paul will make glowing comments on Denny the person and Denny the musician. Their personal and musical partnership has lasted ever since the first Wings and, of course, Denny was the principal musician, apart from the McCartneys, for the album, **Band On The Run**.

If Paul has one pet hate, it's the fear of becoming a business person – someone who goes into the office each day. He told Peter Harvey of *Record Mirror* 'I remember finding myself one day on the phone and suddenly thinking, "Jesus Christ I've been on this phone all day". So you know I thought, I'm either gonna do this for ever, or something else. So I rang the Laine up.' And he proposed that they should get together and form a band.

For Paul and Linda, life is music, life is the family and life is their love. And for them, it works.

Paul has style. Wherever he goes it goes with him – whether it is a local folk-costume or a Hollywood bow tie to greet veteran film star, Gene Kelly. There are always celebrities at a Wings concert.

BEHIND THE ALBUMS

This section covers the two McCartney solo albums, as well as those of Wings, from the release of **Wild Life**.

McCartney:
Apple PCS 7102. Release date: April, 1970
The Lovely Linda; That Would Be Something; Valentine Day; Every Night, Hot As Sun; Glasses; Junk; Man We Was Lonely; Oo You; Momma Miss America; Teddy Boy; Singalong Junk; Maybe I'm Amazed; Kreen-Akore
The first album of solo Paul McCartney, not too well received by the critics, was recorded on a Studer four-track machine using only one microphone. Its very informal nature upset some writers who might have been more interested in the material if it had been adorned with elaborate studio tricks – though, oddly enough, one of the criticisms of the following L.P., **Ram**, was that it seemed nothing but studio gimmickry! McCartney says he didn't exactly sweat over making it but contends that there is much more about this album than some critics were willing to concede. With hindsight, Paul says people now appreciate the album's spontaneity, even the small blemishes, like the sound of doors opening, a tape being spooled back, kids screaming. Certainly it was successful in chart terms for it reached number one in the US charts and two in the British listing. Without doubt, **McCartney** reflected the kind of lifestyle which Paul has elected for himself. It was a family-style production, easy and relaxed. Considerable secrecy surrounded its making and Paul said it was made mostly at his home. He described the music as stemming from 'little bits and pieces, including tunes and melodies from five years ago.' In an interview with *Rolling Stone*, Paul described how he played everything on the album and, in a roundabout way, fulfilled an urge to play lead guitar. In fact, he played just about everything – drums, organ, bongos, acoustic guitar. He said he had gained particular pleasure by working through this album with his wife.

Ram
Apple PAS 1000. Release date: May 1971
Too Many People; 3 Legs; Ram On; Dear Boy; Uncle Albert-Admiral Halsey; Smile Away; Heart Of The Country; Monkberry Moon Delight; Eat At Home; Long Haired Lady; Ram On; The Back Seat Of My Car.
McCartney's **Ram** was hardly the critics favourite album of the month and nor has it had particularly flattering reviews since.

The American section of Apple took from the disc **Back Seat Of My Car** with **Uncle Albert & Admiral Halsey** as a single and it made number one. **Ram** itself presumably charmed the public, if not the music critics. In Britain's trade paper, *Music Week*, which uses the same chart as the BBC,

Ram entered, without fuss, at the top. So at least Paul couldn't complain about the way he was being badly received by the record-buying public, though some did wonder whether the high sales were merely a hangover from Beatle days. The musical reviewers subjected **Ram** to some considerable scrutiny. There was one who said the album sounded more Beatle-ish than a McCartney solo outing. He found a **Hey Jude**-style ending in **Long Haired Lady** and touches of the Abbey Road finale in **The Back Seat Of My Car**. But Paul had never denied he was anything other than an ex-Beatle, and, in view of this, an overnight musical revolution was hardly likely. Another writer thought there was a Beach Boys feel about the shuffle sound of **Back Seat Of My Car** and the same trait could be discerned in **Eat At Home**. Lon Goddard, reviewer at the time for Britain's weekly pop paper, *Record Mirror*, commented that Paul and Linda sounded as close together vocally as the Everly Brothers ever were. **Ram** was very much more than **McCartney**, the husband and wife team. Linda's vocals are in evidence from the beginning of the record. **Ram**, like **McCartney**, suggested cosy domesticity but, then again, Paul never claimed that it was anything else. The cover on this album, like that of **McCartney**, expressed this feeling. **McCartney** had Paul with baby on its back sleeve, while **Ram** had Paul fondling the animal on the front and a family pose with Linda and two children on the flip. Art work was by Paul and photographs by Linda, though one would have thought the latter hardly ranks as one of her all-time greats. This time, though, instead of Paul playing all the musical instruments, some New York session men were used. Paul defended **Ram**, as he had defended **McCartney**, against the critics and, after all, there were good sales.

Ringo was none too flattering. He had not enjoyed **McCartney** and he did not like **Ram**. First and foremost he expressed his belief that Paul was a brilliant artist but the two solo albums revealed only a shadow of the real man. Ringo felt Paul was wasting his time. **Ram**, he thought, contained not one worthwhile tune; there were just some interesting lines. Ringo felt Paul was becoming somewhat strange, almost hiding away from himself the fact that he could write great tunes.

George Martin was pre-occupied with Paul the song-writer. He said in an article written for *Melody Maker* by Richard Williams, 'I don't think Linda is any substitute for John Lennon'. But Paul was happy and he had a gold disc for **Ram** to assure him that a million people or more thought he was doing fine.

Wild Life:
Apple PCS 7152. Release date: November 1971
Mumbo; Bip Bop; Love Is Strange;

Wild Life; Some People Never Know; I Am Your Singer; Tomorrow; Dear Friend.
Wild Life was the first album from McCartney's new band, Wings. The band's line-up was Paul, bass and vocals; Linda, keyboards; Denny Laine, guitar; Denny Seiwell on drums. The album, unlike the previous Paul McCartney solo outings, was given an extra-special publicity fanfare. A party was held at London's Majestic Ballroom and the album was played to journalists and other media people at EMI's famous Abbey Road studios, ahead of release. Afterwards Paul talked with people from his seat at the control board of Studio 2. He said the album took two weeks to make, with most songs accepted on first and second takes. Paul said the object was to achieve a 'live feel' and it was his deliberate intent for the record to have rocking music on side one and slower, more melodic material on the second. He compared the idea to a party; fast music when people arrive, getting less frantic as they get to know each other. McCartney said he had envisaged an album with a generally loose and free atmosphere. And certainly, at least one musical authority saw it more-or-less the way Paul intended. Gavin Petrie of *Disc and Music Echo* said his impression from one hearing was of a disc with 'an appealing mixture of fun and melody and excitement'. This seems to have been the opinion of the British and American public, though chart positions of just inside the Top 10 were not as good as for **Ram**. Other people have not been so impressed and their dissatisfaction with the material was often put in strong terms. The *New Musical Express Encyclopedia of Rock* carries the comment, '. . . the band's first album release, **Wild Life**, was really tepid and showed McCartney's credibility sinking fast.'

Paul had, and still has, considerable affection for this album and, in a conversation with BBC D.J. Paul Gambaccini, he spoke of Dylan being in part inspirational for the idea behind the album – the quick take with sometimes not even time for a sound balance. McCartney also called **Tomorrow**, 'a real big song'. No album cuts found their way into 45 form and chart position, either in Britain or in the States.

Wings – Wild Life certainly did seem a strange way of launching a new group, particularly in view of the considerable publicity which attended the event. Obviously a good strong single would have worked wonders, both for making people aware of McCartney's new project and also ensuring increased album sales. And yet the album had no outstanding track, something which even **McCartney** had with the superb **Maybe I'm Amazed**. One questions whether it was the time for such a loosely put-together album. Such a project carries with it an element of risk and, even if done with the purpose of

making people aware of how the band would sound 'live', it still lacked real reason, for Wings would not tour Britain, apart from the initial college and University gigging, until the Spring of 1972. No cut from the album appears on **Wings Over America**.

Red Rose Speedway:
Apple PCTC 251. Released: May, 1973
Big Barn Bed; My Love; Get On The Right Thing; One More Kiss; Little Lamb Dragonfly; Single Pigeon; When The Night; Lou (1st Indian On The Moon); Medley; Hold Me Tight; Lazy Dynamite; Hands Of Love; Power Cut.

At the end of March, 1973, an album taster, **My Love** was issued as a single in the UK and the same process was followed in the US a month later. America was kinder than Britain and **My Love** became a chart topper, spending a month longer in the US Top 20 than in the UK.

Red Rose Speedway was billed in its inner sleeve as 'Paul McCartney and Wings' and some would say it was, in effect, McCartney's third solo effort, following the steps of **McCartney** and **Ram** rather than **Wild Life**. The album was lavishly illustrated with a twelve-page attached booklet. Most of the pictures were in colour and, although several featured Wings in concert, the overwhelming concentration of pictures and text was on Paul. The album featured Henry McCullough on guitar, but the most interesting thing musically on this album was the prominance of Paul McCartney, bass player. America loved the disc and it shot into number one position in the *Billboard* Hot 200. For a time, it and the compilation album, **Beatles 1967–1970** were back-to-back number ones. In the UK **Red Rose Speedway** entered at six on the week beginning May 19. The same week saw the **Beatles 1967–1970** and the **Beatles 1962–1966** at two and three respectively.

The album received several promotional benefits in Britain, for there was a Wings tour gathering momentum from May 11 and on the previous day there was a British national TV spectacular entitled **James Paul McCartney.**

Red Rose Speedway showed a McCartney searching for the right sound and feel and, while it was better than **Wild Life**, it was still far from his peak. But most critics agreed it was an improvement on previous efforts. What disappointed more than most, perhaps, lay in this album's song material sounding rather ineffectual. McCartney had shown a return of his song-writing ability with a December 1972 single, **Hi Hi Hi** coupled with **C Moon** and it was the flip which attracted most praise. Not that critics have agreed on **Hi! Hi! Hi!** The Carr-Tyler team termed it a 'catchy, inoffensive rocker', while Stephen Barnard from two years after saw it as a 'solid, well sustained rocker' which, according

to him, became a standard for pub rock groups and a disco favourite. But Barnard found **Red Rose Speedway** a progression rather than regression.

Band On The Run;
Apple PAS 10007. Release date: December 1973
Band On The Run; Jet; Bluebird; Mrs. Vandebilt; Let Me Roll It; Mamunia; No Words; Picasso's Last Words (Drink To Me); Nineteen Hundred and Eighty Five.
Band On The Run was the work of Paul, Linda and Denny Laine. Denny Seiwell and Henry McCullough had left just before it was due to be recorded. This time most critics were wild with delight. The public spoke with the same voice and **Band On The Run** was a number one on both sides of the Atlantic. The American release had an extra track, **Helen Wheels**, which had been released as a UK single in November.

The disc became Wings' first platinum album (the others had gained gold status) and from it came two successful singles, **Jet** and the title track. **Jet** reached number seven on both sides of the Atlantic, while **Band On The Run** achieved top rating in Britain and three in America. The record cover attracted immediate attention. There, in spotlight, against what seemed to be a prison wall, were various British celebrities from parliament, television, pop and sport. They appeared very much 'on the run'.

Band On The Run saw Paul on drums and Denny take lead guitar. Paul said he noticed Stevie Wonder had just made several albums playing drums so, since he was faced with a band having no drummer, he decided he might have a go! Much of the album was recorded in Lagos with orchestral backings recorded later in London by Tony Visconti at Air studios. At long last Paul had produced a disciplined album which brimmed with melody and contained plenty of fire and drive. The lyrics had some of McCartney's inscrutability but, like the mystery song of old days, **Hey Jude**, it had that special something. It sparkled with verve and drive, especially so in the shouting unison on the word 'Jet'. The album had ideas, it had variety and a number of its songs could have become hit singles. It was a world away from the sterility of the **Wild Life** album. Most saw this album as going a long way toward establishing once more Paul McCartney's musical standing, at least in the eyes of music critics.

Several songs, apart from **Band On The Run** and **Jet**, caught people's attention. There was the cut, **Let Me Roll It**. This was seen as McCartney's reply to Lennon's nasty swipes at him on the **Imagine** album. McCartney adopted some of Lennon's vocal mannerisms and even included a whimper at the end of the track. It was very much a gentle Paul replying to the sentiments

of **How Do You Sleep?**

The song **Picasso's Last Words** involved American actor, Dustin Hoffman. He and Paul were both holidaying in Jamaica and had met by accident. They met further and Hoffman showed McCartney a cutting he had seen in *Time* magazine, about Picasso's death, which had a poetic ring to its writing. It contained Picasso's last words before he retired to bed for the last time. Hoffman thought the words, 'Drink to me, drink to my health, you know I can't drink any more' was a memorable parting remark from this life. Paul said he strummed some guitar chords and Hoffman was quite amazed to see his idea taking musical form so quickly and memorably.

For Wings and Paul, **Band On The Run** was the confidence-builder they so badly needed. Paul had turned up trumps; gone were the frills and what had, in former albums, been no more than playing around with ideas. Instead here was real development and material which would stand in good stead for the future, as, indeed, was shown by its popularity during the

Wings World Tour of 1975–1976. And it was quite remarkable that the album was made at all. In the first place Wings had been reduced to three only hours before the band was ready for its flight to Lagos. And, secondly, Paul initially met some bad vibes when he arrived in Africa. It seems that some thought he had come to steal genuine African music and use it for his own purposes. Paul's basic reason for going was quite simple. An album needed a studio, that was obvious, and he thought it fun to go and record in an entirely different setting. Perhaps the various difficulties had their effect in giving him a sense of urgency which had been missing for some time from his recordings in album field.

Venus and Mars:
Capitol PCTS 254. Released: May 1975
Venus and Mars; Rock Show; Love In Song; You Gave Me The Answer; Magneto and Titanium Man; Letting Go; Venus and Mars; Spirits of Ancient Egypt; Medicine Jar; Call Me Back Again; Listen To What The Man Said; Treat Her Gently – Lonely Old People; Crossroads.

The less well-disposed musical critics called this '**Band On The Run** revisited'. Whatever the case, Paul and Wings triumphed once more in the charts as this, like its predecessor, topped the album listings in both Britain and America. As with **Band On The Run**, the album had a number of songs which could easily be hit singles. There were strong numbers like **Letting Go, Listen To What The Man Said**, the title track itself, **Rock Show** and **Magneto And Titanium Man**, and some deliciously slow, contemplative tracks like **Treat Her Gently – Lonely Old People**, and the 1920s-sounding, **You Gave Me The Answer**. To dismiss the album as a mere re-take seems hardly fair and McCartney himself saw this L.P. as final proof that things were at last really going well for him.

As for the title, there were those who thought **Venus and Mars** must be Paul and Linda. However, according to Paul, the song found its derivation in the common superstition that people form relationships only if the star signs are favourable. At the time of the album's preparation McCartney was busily delving into Marvel comics and science fiction material. However he had denied that any significant reading of planetary systems and their courses was intended with the album. Similarly, when he talked about his **Rock Show** section, which takes up considerable space on side one of **Venus and Mars**, he denied there existed any deep significance behind certain words and phrases. Paul usually seems much more content to say he writes by playing around with words. Sometimes when they fit there is no obvious sense, other than the pure sound of the words. He has always maintained the best way of writing a song is for it to write itself. He will often have a tune revolving around in his head and then spend days searching for the right words. He maintains there is no proper and correct system and if someone finds themselves being gradually drawn into a routine, then, in his opinion, they should find another way, and quickly. But for all that, McCartney's lyrics on this album and **Band On The Run**, while functional, do not reach anywhere near the heights achieved during Beatle days. They are adequate, but there is little which makes the listener sit up in surprise, perhaps because, unlike **Strawberry Fields** and **Eleanor Rigby** there are fewer figures of speech and the lyrics are more straightforward. **Venus and Mars**, like **Band On The Run**, and indeed the previous albums, lacks the imaginative and arresting lyrics, well laced with unusual images. It shows no sign of the wildness or the craziness of Beatle numbers like **I Am The Walrus**. There, words like 'tee shirt', 'Cornflake' and 'eggman' seemed quite at home in a way in which 'telly' and 'phone' do not in **Spirits Of Ancient Egypt**.

Venus and Mars is a good album, for its music carries the day and cloaks even some of the rather ordinary lyrics with acceptability. For Wings, it was the first album with the group which has lasted into 1977, Paul, Linda, Denny, Joe English and Jimmy McCulloch. It also came with a magnificent front cover, beautifully photographed by Linda. The cover design and Linda's photography deservedly won the 'Album Cover of the Year' award for 1975, given by Britain's music industry journal, *Music Week*.

Wings At The Speed Of Sound:
Parlaphone PAS 10010. Release date: April 1976.
Let 'Em In; The Note You Never Wrote; She's My Baby; Beware My Love; Wino Junko; Silly Love Songs; Cook Of The House; Time To Hide; Must Do Something About It; San Ferry Anne; Warm And Beautiful.
There were two hit singles on this 1976 album, **Let 'Em In** and **Silly Love Songs**, each of which opened respective

sides of the album. In the *Billboard* best sellers of 1976, **Silly Love Songs** accumulated most chart points and so it was named the number one American single of the year. The album was placed third with Fleetwood Mac's self-titled album and Peter Frampton's, **Frampton Comes Alive** being above it in placing. In the United Kingdom, **Silly Love Songs** was placed at 23 with **Let 'Em In** six places lower down, at 29. **Wings At The Speed Of Sound** was placed fourth in the top 50 album listing and apart from two 'Greatest Hits' albums, only one LP of new material from Demis Roussos separated them from the top placing.

With tracks by Jimmy McCulloch and Denny Laine, **Wings At The Speed Of Sound** expressed the growing identity of Wings as a group. For once there had been no personnel changes between albums.

Paul was, of course, still very much to the fore and his songwriting ability and production skill are shown at near best on the opening tracks of both sides of this disc. **Let 'Em In** is McCartney excelling in his ability at selling the understatement. The track could pass as a pleasant piece of inconsequential nothing and, indeed, several reviewers expressed this as their opinion. McCartney at his best is a songwriter whose music suddenly becomes meaningful after a number of hearings, unlike some, whose songs are forgotten after an initial ecstatic reaction. **Let 'Em In** has superb musical feel, a shuffling beat and a simple yet effective lyric theme. There is repeated knocking at a house door and the visitors who come and are let in vary from Sister Susie to Phil and Don Everly to Martin Luther King and Paul's Uncle Ernie. McCartney sings splendidly, as he also does on **Silly Love Songs**. **Silly Love Songs** is McCartney the dreamer who dares to dream in a world which apportions sense only to the hard realist.

On the album, apart from Denny and Jimmy writing songs, there are lead vocals from Denny on **The Note You Never Wrote** and the musically exciting **Time To Hide** and from Jimmy **Wino Junko**, plus Linda on **Cook Of The House** and Joe English is to the fore on **Must Do Something About It.**

The album itself was recorded in several stages, September of 1975 and then again early in 1976. McCartney at a press conference in March of '76, just prior to the band's departure for Copenhagen and their first tour dates of the year, talked of his desire for increasing the group's participation. He said he thought it a good idea to involve Joe, and everyone had been pleasantly surprised to find Joe had such a good voice. Paul said the band had enjoyed making the album, more so because they felt they were now contributing as a group, rather than merely complementing the boss!

Linda's **Cook Of The House**, Paul said, was deliberately given an American high-school feel, the kind of pop music which was around when his wife was in her teens. As for the backing, Paul said, 'The first British cooking on record'. One attractive feature of the album was the subtly different musical introductions to the various tracks; indeed as Paul said, when commenting on the total group participation in the record, 'It's always the object of anything I do, to try and get out of a rut and do something different.' Jimmy McCulloch thought the album had variety with no unduly lengthy cuts. He was pleased for Linda and thought her song was the right kind of tribute to her ability with chips, bacon, red beans and rice, a skill which had enlivened many a breakfast-time. His own song, **Wino Junko**, had some uncomfortable vocal moments and he believed its lyrics had a message for any who might foolishly be contemplating a way of life which has meant disaster for so many young people. For him, one of the album's best songs was Paul's, **Warm And Beautiful**. He thought it would make a good half of a double A-sided disc. Above all, though, he was pleased with the way the band was developing. Jimmy said the band was very settled and they were now entering a peak period. **Wings At The Speed Of Sound** was, in his view, as good an example of this as ever could be found.

But there's no pleasing some people and for professional Wings hater, American writer, R. Meltzer, this was yet another pretty hopeless effort. In his picturesque way, he called it, 'homogenously tinkle-tinkle', and added that it was more like Percy Faith or the Ray Charles Singers, plus an 'intrusive dose of English accent'.

Some general facts about the album should be noted. Linda designed the album cover and once more Wings had a phenomenal seller. In this instance two singles were released after the album. Paul said he thought it a good idea to see which tracks people liked best. At the time of his speaking (in March) he felt **Silly Love Songs** looked a very strong candidate for single release. His own favourite was **Warm and Beautiful**, the last song on the album.

Wings Over America:
PCSP 720 OC 154 – 98 497/8/9. Released: December 1976
Venus and Mars; Rock Show; Jet; Let Me Roll It; Spirits Of Ancient Egypt; Medicine Jar; Maybe I'm Amazed; Call Me Back Again; Lady Madonna; The Long And Winding Road; Live And Let Die; Picasso's Last Words; Richard Cory; Bluebird; I've Just Seen A Face; Blackbird; Yesterday; You Gave Me The Answer; Magneto And Titanium Man; Go Now; My Love; Listen To What The Man Said; Let 'Em In; Time To Hide; Silly Love Songs; Beware My Love; Letting Go; Band On The Run; Hi Hi Hi; Soily.
Wings ended their world tour with the release of a three-record set entitled **Wings Over America**. It was a permanent memento of a great tour and packed with fine performances. The band had now the same line-up from early 1975 and Jimmy McCulloch's words at the time of **Wings At The Speed Of Sound** that they were playing with a new-found freedom here received their vindication.

Obviously criticism of some post-Beatle McCartney lyrics which were made about the **Band On The Run** album still stands; in any case most of the songs on **Wings Over America** come from previously-issued albums, and yet such is the musicianship, the band's tightness aided by a marvellous horn section, such is the quality of McCartney's vocals that even these criticisms tend to pale in the face of a band playing at its peak.

30 sets of tapes were taken and the best was chosen from various venues. There was some cleaning-up, sometimes a studio overdub, particularly if a riff sounded distorted or a vocal harmony a little too far-off mike. In the end, the tapes yielded two hours music.

No details are available about where various cuts had their live birth and, with endless editing, one wonders in any case whether anyone really kept check!

Apart from specfic Wings material, the disc has the Denny Laine solo spot, **Go Now**, the acoustic set, and Paul's popular Beatle medley of **Yesterday, Lady Madonna, The Long And Winding Road, Blackbird** and **I've Just Seen A Face**. Also included is Paul Simon's, **Richard Cory**.

Denny Laine called the world tour, plus the live album, the 'end of Wings phase one', leaving open only the question of where a group travels after reaching such a peak. The only pity about **Wings Over America** is that its very late 1976 release-date deprives it of valuable chart points and sales for the final tally at the end of 1977.

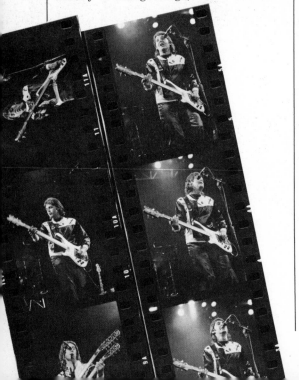

DISCOGRAPHY

This discography lists records made by Paul McCartney, Paul McCartney and Wings, Paul and Linda McCartney, and Wings.

Singles

Record title		Highest chart position as given in Britain by Music Week, and in America by Billboard.
Another Day	U.K.	2
	U.S.A.	5
Uncle Albert/Admiral Halsey	U.S.A.	1
Give Ireland Back To The Irish	U.K.	16
Mary Had A Little Lamb	U.K.	9
Hi Hi Hi/C Moon	U.K.	5
Hi Hi Hi	U.S.A.	10
My Love	U.K.	9
	U.S.A.	1
Live And Let Die	U.K.	9
	U.S.A.	2
Helen Wheels	U.K.	12
	U.S.A.	10
Jet	U.K.	7
	U.S.A.	1
Band On The Run	U.K.	3
	U.S.A.	1
Junior's Farm	U.K.	3
	U.S.A.	16
Listen To What The Man Said	U.K.	6
	U.S.A.	1
Letting Go	U.K.	41
	U.S.A.	—
Silly Love Songs	U.K.	2
	U.S.A.	1
Let 'Em In	U.K.	2
	U.S.A.	1
Maybe I'm Amazed (from Wings Over America)	U.K.	*released Feb. 4, 1977

Albums

Record title		Highest chart position as given in Music Week (U.K.) and Billboard (U.S.A.)
McCartney	U.K.	2
	U.S.A.	1
Ram	U.K.	1
	U.S.A.	2
Wild Life	U.K.	8
	U.S.A.	10
Red Rose Speedway	U.K.	5
	U.S.A.	1
Band On The Run	U.K.	1
	U.S.A.	1
Venus And Mars	U.K.	1
	U.S.A.	1
Wings At The Speed Of Sound	U.K.	2
	U.S.A.	1
Wings Over America	U.K.	9*
	U.S.A.	1*

*position taken from highest placing attained by January 29, 1977.

Songs by Paul McCartney written for other artists.
Mine For Me—Rod Stewart
Catchcall—Chris Barber Jazz Band
Let's Love—Peggy Lee
Penina—Carlos Mendes
Six O'Clock—Ringo Starr
Ten Years After On Strawberry Jam—Scaffold
Liverpool Lou—Scaffold
McGear—the album with Mike McGear, Paul's brother.
Bridge On The River—Country Hams
4th of July—John Christie
Come And Get It—Badfinger
Sweet Baby—Mike McGear
The Family Way—Movie soundtrack

Acknowledgements

The publishers would like to thank the following organizations and individuals for their kind permission to reproduce the photographs in this book:

Camera Press 9 below, 12 below right, 16, 29 centre left, 48-49, 48-49 inset, (David Appleby) 29 centre right, (Tom Blau) 12 above left, (Tom Hanley) 29 above left, (Heilemann) 17, (Charles Hyman) 41 above centre (John Kelly) 14 below, (Linda McCartney) 18-19, (Les Wilson) 20 below left, 90-91; Andre Csillag 72-73, 84-85 below, 89 inset above; Ian Dickson 38-39, 39 below; David Warner Ellis 68 above; Tom Hanley 79; John Hillelson Agency (Andanson/Sygma) 76-77, 78 inset, 82-83; Kelly 80-81; Paul Kemp 86-87; Keystone Press Agency 18 above, 46-47, 50 below, 50-51; Kobal Collection 12-13; London Features International 55, 56, (Neil Jones) 20 above left, 34-35, (Neal Preston) 4-5, 42-43, 66-67, (Mike Putland) 32, 32-33, 35 below, 36-37, 52, 84-85, 91 inset, (Claude Van Heye) 10-11, 40 above, 57, (Chris Walter) 22-23, (Richard Young) 40 below; Michael N. Marks, Creem 58-59, 63 inset, 64-65, 65, 70-71, 72 below right, 74 right, 75, 89 inset below, 92, 93; Barry Plummer, 60-61, 68-69 below, Popperfoto 14 above, 26 below, 78; Press Association 6-7; David Redfern Photography (David Ellis) 27 above; Rex Features Ltd 12 below left, 15, 16-17, 21 right, 24-25, 26-27, 28 above, 29 above right, 29 below, 30-31, 31 above and below, 41 below left, 45 below right, 49 below right, 49 right, 66, 68-69 above, 72 left, 89; Rolling Stone Magazine 62-63, 82; S.K.R. Photos International Ltd 8-9; Joseph Stevens 41 right, 83; Syndication International 53, 54; Chris Walter endpapers, 28 below, 74 left.